FIND OUT
FOR
YOURSELF

Young People Can Discover Their Own Answers

EUGENIA PRICE

TURNER
PUBLISHING COMPANY

Turner Publishing Company
Nashville, Tennessee
www.turnerpublishing.com

Cover design: Bruce Gore

Library of Congress Cataloging in Publication Data Upon Request

9781684425808 paperback
9781684425815 hardcover
9781684425822 eBook

17 18 19 20 10 9 8 7 6 5 4 3 2 1

Contents

1. Finding Out for Yourself 5

2. Finding Out About Yourself 11

3. Finding Out About Your Talents. 17

4. Finding Out About Your Tastes 24

5. Finding Out About Your Prejudices 31

6. Finding Out About God 38

7. Finding Out What You Really Believe . . . 44

8. Finding Out How to Be With God 51

9. Finding Out God's Idea for Your Life . . . 58

10. Finding Out About Real Popularity 65

11. Finding Out About Your Parents 71

12. Finding Out About People 80

13. Finding Out About Christian Conduct 87

14. Finding Out About Guilt 95

15. Finding Out About Fear 104

16. Finding Out About Your Real Potential . . . 115

Preface

In *Find Out For Yourself* I have written what I deeply hope will be sixteen chapters of frank, open *stimulation* to you, if you are young. The writing, I confess, has been that to me, and I am no longer even pretending to be young!

In these pages it is my intention that you be stimulated to *think through* the basic issues involved in living *your* life, with your background, your education, your hopes and ideals. Of one thing I am certain: young people can think, and I believe you want to do much more thinking for yourself than you have been encouraged to do. I have not attempted to arrive at conclusions for you. What good are my pat conclusions, when it is your life you must live?

Some of my own thinking is, of course, shared with you, and some of my own experience. You will find some recognizable experiences of other people your age, too. But *Find Out For Yourself* has *not* been written *down* to any age — it has been written with full respect for your innate *and* academically sharpened intelligence. To some of you, parts of it may seem simple, obvious; to others, certain sections will seem overly adult. May I ask a favor of all of you? Before you decide either way, will you read the entire book? I ask you neither to overestimate, nor underestimate yourself. I have certainly meant to do neither.

Among the many ways in which the adults in your world have let you down, perhaps one of the most harmful is the fact that we have underestimated your ability to *think*. I plead "not guilty" to this one, anyway. I dare you to think with me, through every page!

Eugenia Price

Chicago, Illinois
May 1, 1963

1 *Finding Out for Yourself*

"All right, go ahead — find out for yourself!" This old parental stand-by is usually spoken with finality, some desperation, and almost invariably implies: All right, go ahead — find out the *worst* for yourself. Find out that I'm right and you're wrong. Find out that what you're determined to do is bad, futile, unwise, wasteful — or any of several familiar *negatives*.

With all respect to your elders whom you may have provoked into this helpless kind of outburst, I must make it clear that I have no intention whatever of pointing you toward any *negative* discoveries. Discovery is natural to young people, but why concentrate on negative discovery when an entire life of positives stretches before you? Chapter by chapter in this book we will be attempting to help you free yourself to the point of finding out — *not* that you're probably heading for disaster if you insist upon thinking for yourself, but that you *must* begin right now to do your own thinking if you are to discover life at its best for *you*.

In no way does this mean you are to think altogether independently of other people. Total independence (or the desire for it) is characteristic of the young teen-ager. As you mature, you become interested in *inter-dependence:* learning to act and react *with* other people; learning to weigh their thinking against your own, and choose the combination of ideas which seems wisest to you in the light of what you have thought through for yourself. Children are not yet able to think entirely for themselves, and so parents are generally satisfied to teach them to obey without thinking, oftentimes to their harm. Every human being should begin as early as possible to think things through for himself, and it is right here that I believe we as adults do great wrong to young people. We supply you with what we consider answers through your childhood years and into your teens — then suddenly we expect you to take off overnight into full-blown maturity. It is a pet theory of mine that we often expect too much of you intellectually and not enough of you emotionally. What better way to split you in two and add to your department of utter confusion?

5

We support laws that force you to expose your intellects to twelve to sixteen years of daily education. Your report cards from school assume maximum importance. You spend hours in school in the classroom and more hours at home poring over big stacks of books. There is peace between you and your parents or teachers only if you are making good marks. You feel a "success" only if the report card shows you are mastering subjects that would make your parents' heads swim! When you graduate from high school, those of you who enter college are expected to think through courses that would really bend the brain of the average adult. Current college curricula require concentration and analysis arrived at only by strenuous mental labor and acumen. The high school and college student is no longer spoon-fed his three R's. He is expected to think for himself, to deduce, to draw valid conclusions. The high school graduate who enters business finds himself suddenly in a world of adults, with new and often heavy responsibilities which carry their weight of problems to solve and decisions to be made. Those who marry young are faced abruptly with human relationship tangles and household management, and sooner or later they are in the difficult position of creating an atmosphere of security for their children.

If we are realistic, it would seem that almost overnight you are expected to be mature people. I have no argument with the necessity of your growing up — becoming a mature personality. That, *per se*, is the point of this book. Our world is in its present condition of turmoil mainly because many of its so-called adults in power are brilliant and educated, but basically immature, self-centered, impetuous people. When the leaders of major nations lose their tempers, and bang their shoes on the peace tables, can anyone by the wildest stretch of the imagination call them mature human beings?

Maturity is (or should be) the goal of every person born into our world. Still, I am firmly convinced that saddling young people with gigantic intellectual and academic problems is not enough. We expect big things of you mentally, and only half enough emotionally. We stimulate your intellects and cripple your emotions by supplying you with higher education and continuing to treat you as emotional babies.

Your intellects grow only as they are stimulated to grow,

and this we do. But what about your total personalities? What about your emotions? Are we stimulating you to grow emotionally? To learn to make your own decisions? To assume the responsibilities someone else assumed for you when you were children? You are expected to be near mental giants in school, but do your parents and teachers still expect you to take their word for your religious beliefs? Your personal conduct? Your choices?

Have you really begun to think things through for yourself? Or are you still acting on someone else's opinion? As long as adults go on doing your personal thinking for you, you will remain one-sidedly immature, no matter how high your grades are in school, or how successful you are in your job. If you are still acting on the opinions of other people, your convictions will not be strong enough to hold you in the crisis times — and make no mistake about it, crisis times come to us all.

What about your faith in God? Is it your own? Or is it your parents' faith warmed over by your desire to please? What about your talents? Are you developing the talent you know to be your best? Or are you embarking on a career of your parents' choosing? What about your tastes? Are they truly yours? Or have they been dictated by some well-meaning adult who wants to be able to say: "Your taste is just like mine, dear!" If it is, fine. But is it really? No virtue involved either way, but you will find life for yourself *only* if you have found your true self first. What about your prejudices? Do you have them? And if so, are they truly your own? Or did your family form them for you during the years in which you were not thinking for yourself, and do you perhaps now find them just so much excess baggage?

We will go into all of these interesting aspects of *you* in later chapters, but for now, concentrate on discovering just how much you have begun to think things through for yourself. Have you learned to think clearly in the areas *not* directly connected with your academic world or your job? Have you been encouraged by anyone to use the same intellectual agility in the problem areas of your emotional life that you have learned to use in drawing right conclusions or correct analyses in your most difficult courses at school? Have you thought through your own personal belief in God?

7

Or your lack of it? Do you follow certain behavior patterns or prohibitions simply because you have always done so? Or do you have sound reasons for living as you live? Has it ever occurred to you that the same good brain that works for you in the chemistry lab can go to work for you in the areas of creative conduct? Are your religious belief and your philosophy of life your own? If they turn out to be the same as your parents' views, well and good. But are they yours? Have you thought them through for yourself? Do you know why you make the choices you make? Do you assume responsibility for a valid reason, or just to please someone older on whom you may still be financially and emotionally dependent?

Our world is full of young people with excellent minds, who make good grades in their studies, but who suddenly turn stupid when it comes to living. For that matter, our world is full of adults in the same predicament. Whose fault is this?

After all, adults were young once, too. Is their chronic state of wasted energy, bitterness, anxiety and worry entirely their own doing? Or did someone older than they fail to urge them to begin using their minds when they were your age?

What about the young people who spend money and time and energy trying to "live it up," but still carry deep inside them big loads of fear and guilt and drift off to sleep at night feeling lost and inadequate? If you do not learn to think through to the real issues now, how can you be expected to learn later? You are setting your life patterns *now*. Not tomorrow — now. What you are now, you will be later — only more so.

Of course, as you grow older, you will (or you can) increase your ability to think, but right now is the important time. Adults use a lot of clichés which bore you, but young people use a few which make us a little tired, too. One of them is the old stand-by: "Oh, I didn't *think*." It is natural for you to slip up sometimes because you're young. But you can make yourself far more attractive to everyone concerned, if you begin now to make *thinking* a habit. Far from being a dull thing to do, it will give you that freedom you crave more quickly than any other path you might follow.

I was wakened not long ago a little before 2 A.M. by

8

a loud roar of wide-open automobile motors in the street outside my house. I sleep soundly, but two "souped-up jobs," minus mufflers, driven at high speed down a normally quiet residential street in the middle of the night, jerked me to my feet in time to see one of the two cars pass the other and crash into one, then two, then three parked cars. When the police came, we learned that the drivers of both cars were in their early twenties — each old enough to have *thought through* the danger of drag racing down a two-way city street parked solidly on each side with automobiles belonging to my sleeping neighbors. Both fellows looked stunned and surprised and acted as though the girl who was injured in one of the speeding cars should have ducked in time. Somehow it was her fault — hers, and the arresting policemen, that they were now in a load of trouble.

A few years ago I was standing in line in a college cafeteria in the company of a half dozen Christian students, all reasonably intelligent, attractive kids. We were at the end of the line, talking comfortably, when two highly self-conscious, much made-up gals fell in line behind us. My friends, the Christian students, were suddenly silent. We made our selections without another word, until my curiosity caused me to ask, "What's the trouble? Why all the sudden quiet?"

"Oh, it's those girls back there at the end of the line," a fellow whispered. "They're always trying to horn in on our group and they're no good!"

Now for a question: What did these Christian young people in the college cafeteria have in common with the drag racers who caused the commotion in front of my house in the middle of the night? I did not ask what the drag racers had in common with the two girls at the end of the line labeled "no good" by the Christian group. *What did the Christian students have in common with the drag racers?*

One all-important thing — neither the Christians nor the drag racers were thinking clearly.

It doesn't take an experienced psychologist to decide that the boys who sped down a crowded city street were not using their heads. Little Abner would say, "As any fool can plainly see," they were headed for trouble. But what about the half dozen Christian young people? Nothing catastrophic or illegal was about to occur to them because they were not

9

thinking, *but* if their Christianity had invaded their *minds*, they would have thought through to the crux of the matter. If these two pathetically made-up pagan girls had been trying to "horn in," didn't it stand to reason that they were being pursued by the very Christ these so-called followers worshiped? Weren't these Christians missing a marvelous chance to show the love of Christ to two other young people who obviously hadn't had the benefit of Christian backgrounds? What if the girls were "vulgar," as one of the more pious of the Christian group declared? Did they need to stay that way? Couldn't Christ change them too? Didn't He say, "Come unto Me *all* . . ."?

I had been speaking to these Christian young people about witnessing, and they had listened with profound attention, each one expressing a desire to become a better witness for Jesus Christ. This was at 11:30 A.M. But at noon, less than an hour later, they had all stopped using their brains and were frozen solid against two fellow students, who, if they did not know they longed for Christ, at least were obviously lonely kids.

The drag racers found out for themselves the hard way. If they had been urged to think for themselves first, they could have avoided trouble, injuring no one, leaving my neighbors' cars intact and our sleep undisturbed. It is easy to label as thoughtless those so-called "delinquents" who cause havoc in the middle of the night. But what about the Christians? If young people refuse to use their minds in one area, what is the guarantee they won't refuse in others too? In my opinion, the Christian group injured those two unwanted girls in the cafeteria line just as surely as the drag racers injured the girl in the front seat of one of their roaring cars.

Thinking through — finding out for yourself, is for *now*, not for later. And thinking is not only for avoiding trouble. It is for discovering *life* at its most interesting "best."

2 Finding Out About Yourself

What do you actually mean when you say: "I love to be with that person because he or she *understands* me"?

You can mean one of two things, as I see it: either you are the honest type of person who truly wants to grow and mature, and you are stimulated by the company of the person who sees your faults as well as your good points and still loves you; *or* you have found a satellite who wants so much to please you that he or she agrees with you at every turn, condoning, even complimenting you, no matter what you do or say.

To be understood, however, does not necessarily denote sympathy or even agreement. It seems to me we have rather kicked around the word "understood" almost to the point of making it synonymous with sympathy and a stroked brow. God called Himself *understanding,* and surely He is the only living Person who completely understands each one of us, but this does not mean that God is ready to pat us on the back and go along with our every whim and fancy. *Understanding* someone means *knowing* that person; being able to separate the false motives from the true ones, the deceptions from the truth.

As I understand it, when the theologian speaks of our sinful self, he speaks of our *false* self. When man jerked the reins of his life out of the hands of God and began to orbit independently of his Creator, he began to form his *false* self — a thing other than the true self God created for man in the beginning. Our lives are creative in direct ratio to how much our redeemed (given back) *true* selves are operative day by day. When I, as an adult, first met Jesus Christ, I found, for the first time, *two* selves within me doing battle. This was my newly returned *true self* in opposition to the familiar *false self* which I had nurtured independently of God for thirty-three years. As I am able to recognize the remnants of that old, false (sinful) self still in operation, I can (now that I have His power within me) choose which self is going to win. So can you, if you have received Jesus Christ as your own Saviour. He is just as generous with His power with one as He is with another.

11

We begin to form and cultivate our false selves at an appallingly early age. Here again, the theologian has a name for it: original sin. Try crossing a baby in his crib and see how "christian" he acts! Bad tempered small children have done a great deal more to contribute to my understanding of the nature of man than the combined efforts of the scholars of theology. When a baby doesn't get his way, he screams like a banshee! Why? He was born with a dominant self that wants its own way. He may be screaming for something that will do him great harm, and surely no one expects a baby to know the difference intellectually. But it is when this same dominant self is still screaming in one form or another at your age, or at my age, that we begin to be able to see the big difference between our true selves (given back to us at our redemption, according to God's original plan, through Jesus Christ) and our false selves with which we have grown so familiar.

It is human nature to enjoy the people who agree with us and condone our behavior, whether we are right or wrong. This is still true of me, I hasten to confess. Needless to say, I've had some interesting and provocative criticism since I have dared to write books about living day by day with Christ. Some of the criticism has been extremely helpful. Some has made me chuckle. Some has hurt. But I am human, and I am *I*, and so naturally I feel more comfortable and more deeply "understood" in the company of the type of Christian whose prohibitions, or lack of them, more closely match mine.

I am not arguing right or wrong here, merely that we do feel more at home with the people who agree with us. This is not necessarily right or wrong, it is just human nature. And human nature is not necessarily right or wrong in itself. Our point for now is that we are not *understood* according to our points of agreement. We are understood according to how realistically we are observed.

God is all reality. He embroiders nothing. He exaggerates nothing. He minimizes nothing. He sees us and understands us exactly as we are. This in no way influences His love for us, of course. He does not love you more because you are a Phi Beta Kappa or president of your youth group. He does not love you less if you are a trouble-making rebel.

He understands you exactly as you are and He loves you exactly as He is. He cannot help loving you. He *is* love. He *is* also understanding, and so He cannot help understanding you. You may fool your friend or your parent and increase their love and regard for you. If many of my Christian friends knew me as I am, they would lose about 50 per cent of their regard for me, I have no doubt. Their love and regard for me is greatly influenced by the fact that they believe me to be in practically total agreement with them. We "see things alike," so we get along fine. We do not necessarily "see things" the way God sees them — He warned us that His ways are higher than our ways — but still He bends every effort to keep us in close relationship with Himself.

God does not need to find out about us, He already knows us. As David wrote from his own experience, "Thou hast me in mind when I sit down and when I rise up; Thou discernest my thoughts from afar. Thou hast traced my walking and my resting, and art familiar with *all my ways.*"

God not only understands us, He is *familiar* with us.

He knows us through and through.

Now, doesn't it stand to reason that the more we allow His life (which includes His *knowing*) to be operative in us, the more clearly we will know ourselves? I am 46 years old as I write this chapter in this book, and daily I am finding out more and more about myself; and I make these new discoveries in direct proportion to the control God has over my life. When He came to live His life in me, He brought along His total ability to understand *me* — as I am. Not as I think I am. Not as I wish I were. Not as you think I am, but as I really am.

Lay hold of the fact that you need not go on fooling yourself about you — unless you want to. He will no more force His understanding upon you than He will force His love. God waits for us to choose; but when we do choose to live our lives according to His design and desires for us, He lavishes the needed power and understanding upon us.

Finding out about what you're really like is perhaps the most important step toward maturity and balance. True balance is truly Christian. Jesus Christ was in no way off-balance or eccentric during His years on earth. A Christian man or woman who is "way out" on any one issue is always less of an authentic to me than one who is balanced and on center. There is no way to mature toward balanced, authentic Christian living, however, unless you begin now to find out what you are *really* like. Of equal importance is finding out about God's true nature (see Chapter 6). But there are two of you involved in your life — God and *you*, so the more familiar you become with both, the smoother your progress will be.

Balance is not a dull thing. How far can you go in a high-powered car with only three wheels? Balance gets you there with less bumps and fewer pieces to pick up after yourself. Balance is a thing to be thought about and a state to be much desired. I fail to see how you or anyone else can become balanced, however, until you know yourself. If you are a "way out" personality, face it and learn to live with yourself accordingly. If you are an extremist, admit it, and learn how to make creative use of that tendency toward extremism. If you harness extremism and send it flying in the right direction, it can work for you and not against you. If you are an introvert, don't torture yourself and those around you by trying to whip your naturally quiet personality into that of a rowdy Joe. You are *not* a rowdy Joe. You are *you*. If the wise-cracking girl or fellow is the popular one in your set, let it be. You will only distort what's good and attractive about you by trying to be like someone else. You will only throw yourself off balance.

If you are an extrovert, don't allow the intellectuals you know to cause you to feel inferior because you don't spend hours discussing Nietzsche and Kant. If you prefer to read only *Life* magazine and scan the headlines, face this fact about yourself and begin to be the best headline scanner you know.

I am not suggesting that you *cultivate* your most prominent traits in order to call attention to yourself, but I am urging that you accept yourself as you are and stop trying to be someone else. You can only be the best *you*, never the best *me*. There is no particular virtue involved in either extroversion or introversion. Both extremes should work toward balance, but balance will never come if you make fun of the "people lovers" because you happen to prefer your own company and a good book. If you're a "people lover," and prefer an evening with the gang, you will only become a boor if you criticize and laugh at the girl or fellow who prefers to read alone or discuss the United Nations.

If you are a born leader, don't spoil God's plan for your life by feeling superior to those who stutter when called upon to make an announcement in public. You are *not* necessarily superior — you are just you. The shy, timid, non-leader type is not necessarily inferior, either. People are simply different, and in each personality is some valued God-given trait which can be cultivated to benefit the world in general.

Some of our greatest scientists have been shy and socially diffident men in a group. Leaders do not always have to make noise. If you "ain't got rhythm," don't feel inferior; find out what you do have and make the most of it.

If your parents have been unwise and compared you unfavorably with one of your brothers or sisters or cousins or the fellow or girl next door, don't make the mistake of sinking into an abyss of self-pity; and right now stop resenting your faulty elder. Adults do have faults too, you know, just like you. You shouldn't have been compared unfavorably with anyone; you should have been encouraged to be your best self from the beginning. But if this has happened, realize that someone made a mistake, forgive him or her, and begin right now to find out about *you* as you really are.

In the next chapter, we are going to find out about your talents. But how can you do this if you haven't yet found out about *you*? One discovery follows the other, and if you are throwing yourself off balance by acting on your false self — or a false estimate of yourself — you will go right on along the wrong track where your talents are concerned.

Perhaps one of the best ways to discover yourself, your true self, is to check your self-respect department. How much do you really respect yourself? Christians are often hammered at to "destroy" self. This is not what Jesus said to do. He told us we were to love our neighbors as much as we love ourselves. How can we love a self we have destroyed? Actually, it is not even possible to do away with our *selves*. As long as we *are*, there will be our *selves*. True, we are to place our selves under the control of the Creator God (and who could know better how these selves should function?) but we are not to despise our selves or try to commit self-

15

suicide. We are to be objective and clear-sighted about them and, after linking them to the very Self of God, go on to develop His creation to its maximum.

There is, of course, a right kind of self-love and a wrong kind. If you pamper yourself, you do not really love the essential you. Pampering always hampers. Jesus did not tell us to pamper either ourselves or our neighbors. He spoke of love. And love is creative and realistic and constructive. If we are cultivating our false selves, the self-seeking, self-preserving, distorted self which motivates all selfish behavior, we cannot expect anything but imbalance and bumps. God created man in His own image, and He created him into a human family. Families are supposed to get along together. When they don't, it is because false selves are being cultivated right and left. Each member of the human family has a definite, particular contribution to make to the whole. I have mine, you have yours. When we learn to respect this fact in ourselves, we are then ready to begin to learn to respect it in the people we know.

None of us is perfect. None of us is altogether attractive. We are all on the way, or we can be with Christ out in front. If you as a young person can learn to accept yourself as you are, you will then be able to accept your friends as they are. Once we have begun this realistic walk together, we are well on the way — not to a life without problems, but to a life where we can learn to meet the inevitable problems creatively.

If you hate yourself, something is radically wrong. You may be trying to love a false image someone else has helped you build up. You may be toiling away at the wrong kind of humility. You may be expecting too much of you. You may be trying to imitate someone you admire, not succeeding, and as a consequence, despising yourself. If you are being you, honestly, and cooperating with your parents, teachers, friends and God in developing the best you, you are on the way to real maturity. You may also be expecting not too much, but the wrong things of yourself. Any of these traps are set for us all, but we can avoid them *if* we (at whatever age we see the need and opportunity) find out about our real selves and begin to act realistically on what we discover.

3 Finding Out About Your Talents

One thing we should have straight from the beginning: we can't all be ten-talent people! In fact, if we were, it would be an even more complicated world. Ten-talent people have it rough most of the time. Why? Simply because they are so different from the rest of the human race. They find it more of a problem to adjust to the tempo set by the majority of us who have one or maybe two noticeable talents. Ten-talent people are in the minority, and the majority sets the pace.

So, if you find yourself capable of doing only one or two things well, relax. Life will be less of a disturbance — to your emotions at least. Those few who excel in a half dozen directions or more, understandably find the rest of us somewhat slow, dull, out of step. In a way, though, these few rare ones remind me of the old story about the doting grandmother who, watching her grandson Johnny as he marched along in a parade one day, remarked: "Why, every one of those boys is out of step except Johnny!"

Before we go further, however, if you *are* a ten-talent person, take heart. Life *will* present more difficult adjustment problems for you, but you need not feel "out of step." Your need for emotional balance may be greater, but wherever there is need, there God can really go into operation. For some reason you have come by several unusual gifts. Your life can be blessed or cursed by them. This is your decision mainly. You can allow the insecurity of not being like other people to grow within you, so that you dodge behind a wall of superiority, or you can decide right now that you will always need God in a particular way, and give thanks. Give thanks for your need as well as your talents. Actually, as you grow older, you *may* be one of the fortunate few adults who come to see that nothing is so golden as need! Notice I said you *may* come to see this. Most people don't, despite the fact that Jesus said plainly that those who recognize their need will be doubly blessed. Need alone does not bless us, but our recognition of it can, *if* we turn to Him in that need.

Now, if you sail along making straight A's and excelling in art, music, science and still more, your friends might think

17

you have no needs whatever. They may feel you are so much more fortunate than they, that they eventually convince you. (It is a pronounced human characteristic that we tend to think about ourselves the way most other people think about us. This may or may not be realistic.) In part, if you are many-talented, life will come easier for you. But there is always the other side of the coin to be considered. Simply the fact that you *are* many-talented will no doubt increase your restlessness. When other people exhaust themselves in their effort to do a good job, you will be able to whip it out quickly, with energies and time to spare. Into these unused energies and this unspent time will rush a kind of restlessness. You will try to call it by many names: loneliness, superiority, even inferiority. You may feel unlovable merely because there is no one else around with time or energy enough to get into your spare time with you. They are all still working, or studying or re-doing what you found so simple to accomplish. You will be enthusiastic about many more things because of your natural gifts. Perhaps you will be excited about dramatics, the novel, history, even electronics. Your roommate at school, or the girl or fellow who works with you at your job, may only be interested in athletics. Once more, you can fall into the unrealistic trap of feeling superior, lonely, or again — inferior, because no one can enter in with you.

This is an unrealistic attitude, because you are simply not thinking things through as they are. You have not become well enough acquainted with either yourself or your friends. More than that, you have not accepted yourself as you are, nor them as they are. You and they, perhaps have allowed the competitive spirit to enter into the situation. *Competition* is not the point here. *Cooperation* is the point. Your friends who never seem to have enough time to get things done may feel inferior to you; they may resent your talents. You may answer their misjudging of you by misjudging them in turn. None of this leads to harmony. It all can lead to confusion and hurt feelings and misunderstandings.

If you are a ten-talent person, right now is the best time to accept it, give thanks for the talents — but also give thanks that you have come to see that you will always have to rely more on God for balance and understanding of the other people in your life. Being different is not easy, but the end result comes out about the same if we are realistic about it. Accomplishment will be easy for you and hard for them. But making friends will be hard for you and easy for them, mainly because they are in the majority.

Not long ago I received a letter from a young man of sixteen, already in college. He enclosed some of his poetry and this, along with the contents of his letter, told me quickly that here was perhaps a sprouting genius. I was excited about him, but my heart also went out to the boy. I was to speak soon at the college where he was enrolled. My curiosity ran high and I looked forward to meeting him. Would he be an unattractive eccentric, shunned by the rest of the students? I received a pleasant surprise. In conversation he was even more brilliant than in his letter. *But* – he was with his best friend, a mild-mannered athletic fellow who obviously accepted the multi-talented boy as an equal. I saw at once that my friend, the budding genius, was on top of the situation. He was just as interested in what his friend wanted to do with his life as he was in his own unusual writing ability. He quieted my fears about his adjustment to normal life at once: "Oh, I've thought it all through. If the others think I'm peculiar because I like to take walks alone, then come back and write poems about it, that's all right. They wouldn't be living as their best selves if they tried to be like me, and I have no intention of trying to be like them."

His friend chimed in with, "Yeah, live and let live." They both grinned and so did I. It was all good, healthy, under control. This boy will have problems, but who doesn't? The important thing is that he is *thinking* realistically. He is discovering himself and accepting himself as he is. He is also discovering his friends and he is accepting them as they are. Whether they return his balanced attitude is not his responsibility, it is theirs.

Families often do not understand many-talented young people. In fact, it is rare when they do. One gifted young woman I know is now in New York, "discovering herself." Her family permitted her to go, but they are all fearful, not because she has done shocking things, but because she is so talented and has such a brilliant mind that she has never reacted or even thought along the family norm. She knows

19

God, I believe, in the deep, important way. She refuses to express Him according to the family pattern, so they just look at her and wonder, what next? She is lonely. She has always been lonely, except for one or two older friends who, like me, find her totally stimulating. But she is learning to understand her family, whether they understand her or not, and she is accepting them as they are, recognizing their love for her and their caring. She has lost most of her rebellion by now and is allowing the energy once used up in it to be turned creative. She *is* different, but now it is all right with her. Why? Because she has accepted herself as God accepts her, full of deep need and bright potential.

No one is uncomfortably different with God. He loves the "fringe" people among us with the same unrelenting love as He does the "normal" and run-of-the-mill.

So far we have spoken mainly of the ten-talented people. What about the rest of us? For one thing, if you are not a many-talented person, you should have come to understand yourself better from having read this far in the chapter. The main points still apply: know yourself as you are, and accept yourself realistically. Some of you will feel that you are a no-talented person. This is just not true. There is no such animal. Your talent may not fall into the much-touted groupings — art, science, music, etc., but that in no way means you have no talent. You may not be a public speaker, you may not be able to add, you may have trouble writing a letter or drawing a straight line, but talent does not stop with *doing*. This is why the many-talented oftentimes have a rougher time of it. Real talent is demonstrated best in *being*. One look at the biographies of great artists will show you that most of them lived mainly unhappy, unsuccessful emotional lives. What you *are* is the final criterion, both in this life and for all eternity.

And yet, we do need to earn our living and take our necessary place in this world, so finding out realistically about our talents is of real importance. This chapter and the next, *Finding Out About Your Tastes*, are closely related. Your tastes are among your best guideposts to your talents, so keep this in mind as you read Chapter Four.

God did not mean for our earthly lives to be strained and difficult. Jesus said He came to give us a more abundant life! Too many people think that if we are pleasing God, the whole thing has to be unpleasant, painful, difficult. This is simply not true, and believing it is insulting to God. He did not try to fool us where trouble is concerned. Jesus also said that on this earth we would have plenty of trouble. So we need to balance out what He said, not jump on any one sentence. There will be hours of hard work and days of disappointment as you develop your talents, but His promise about the abundant life holds. Jesus, you see, is always totally *realistic*.

In a book of this scope it would, of course, be impossible to go into vocations or separate talents. But you have plenty of access to help like this. What we must do together here in these pages is learn to think through the subject of talents in relation to your life as a whole, and to you as an individual.

If you excel on some musical instrument and also as a public speaker, you know it and so does everyone who knows you. Should you cultivate and develop both of these talents, or only one, to a high degree of excellence? A good question, and it brings us logically to a big secret which few adults ever learn: the difference between mere *self-expression* and genuine *communication*. Check your talent activity along this line and you may find much of the confusion cleared away at once. When you make use of your talent as a musician, a speaker, a writer, or teacher – are you only expressing yourself or your opinion or your taste, or are you really *getting through* to those who are exposed to your gift? If you're a soprano or tenor and you leave your audience merely gasping at that last clear, high note – is this enough? Is this really reason enough to continue to study, or should there be more? There should be more, of course.

It doesn't take a spiritual geiger counter to discover when a minister stands in his pulpit expressing himself, reaching his congregation only with his ability – his talent. But when a man really *communicates* God from his pulpit, the people who listen know it, and their hearts respond to God, not only to the man standing before them. Two singers may sing about the love of God, using the same lyrics set to the same music, and yet have decidedly different effects on their audiences. One may *communicate* the love of God, the other may *express* his or her talent magnificently. So, if you possess two talents, check yourself here. Even if you only possess one — check yourself. Self-expression is normal to the young, but as you mature, if you are truly mature, you will begin to want to skip the self-expression and begin to communicate.

I am convinced that three-fourths of the people who long to sing, write, act or perform publicly in any of the dozens of acceptable ways, do so because they want to express themselves. Does this sound harsh? Perhaps. And while self-expression is important, lasting self-expression comes only from true communication. Lasting self-expression, in fact, comes as one of the by-products of true communication. The mother who communicates values and love and interest to her children has found the supreme self-expression; but it has not been her primary motive.

Talent is in no way limited to the so-called creative arts. Your talent may lie in mathematics (as creative as any piece of sculpture!). It may lie in the field of engineering, electronics, agriculture, construction, medicine, politics, education, or some branch of Christian ministry. We speak carelessly when we speak of "talented young people" as only those who make some public or artistic display of talent. The root of real talent may lie deep within your being, so deep only the years may free it. You may even think of yourself as a no-talent kid. Don't be that superficial with yourself! Don't be that brutal. Because if you minimize your talents now, you can quickly build up a barrier that will keep them forever penned up inside you.

On the other hand, if you are carried away with your talents, don't be *that* superficial with yourself either! To be utterly self-centered is normal for the young. But you are on your way to maturity now, so watch it. This does not imply that you should stick your light under the proverbial bushel. Far from it. But do begin to think clearly about the deeper dimensions where your talent is concerned. You have the important job of training, guiding and polishing your talent, but what you *communicate* to the rest of the world through that talent is the thing that will give you permanent stimulation and reward.

Art for art's sake has great and lasting merit. At my age, I am still in conflict at times concerning where my first allegiance lies — to write up to my highest artistic ability, or to communicate to the most people. I doubt if anyone who truly loves Jesus Christ has a clear-cut answer here. I know I am still struggling with it. But I do believe that once we choose the level on which we mean to use our talent, we then should train it to its maximum and turn our concentration upon those with whom we wish to communicate. I am not contending that I make it always, but with each book I write I think constantly in terms of who will read it. Here I am attempting to communicate with you at your age, much as we talk when we have met in schools and colleges across the continent. I am not writing this book in order to air a few of my collected thoughts about young people. I am writing it with the hope of communicating with *you*. I am making use of the amount of talent I possess to reach you where you are, in order to involve you to the point of carrying your own thinking beyond these pages.

Your talent may be parenthood. I can think of no more important gift. Can you imagine a greater need for genuine communication than between parents and their children? Has this been lacking in your home? Are you interested in doing something about it when you are one of the two parents in your own home someday? Each of us has been given the talent for communication by the God who communicated His love to the whole human race. If you doubt yours, it could be that you just never have had the freedom and opportunity to try it out.

Be interested in yourself and in your talents. There is nothing wrong with self-interest as long as it is motivated by a genuine desire to become your best self. If you are your best self, with your talents developed to *communicate,* you are bound to make a contribution — not to the world's headache, as do some of those who worship only their talent, but to the world's heartease.

Talents are gifts from God; be thankful for them. But if you seem to be short-changed, think it through before you begin blaming God for being a miser where you are concerned. His ideas and hopes for you are very definite. Think it through before you decide you've been cheated. Give yourself time to discover *you* as you are, down under the possible quirks and foibles and bad breaks. You could be wonderfully surprised at what He has planned — for you.

4 *Finding Out About Your Tastes*

According to my brand new dictionary, *taste*, as we are considering it, means: individual preference, liking, relish, fondness, inclination.

We are all possessors of taste. Everyone is born with certain basic individual preferences, likings, inclinations. At one time I would have said glibly that all children are born with a preference, even a fondness for candy. This, I now know, is not true. My niece, Cindy, simply did not like candy until she went to school and discovered her classmates adored it! This, then, is our first point. We do all come into the world with certain tastes inherent to us. But, more often than not, our tastes are mainly cultivated ones. Now, at the age of nine, Cindy *prefers* candy in a big way.

There is nothing essentially wrong with cultivated tastes. There is nothing essentially right about them either. In themselves, they could be called neutral—until we begin to examine the results or consequences of these indulged tastes.

I would thoroughly enjoy writing for several pages on the necessity for you to see to it that your tastes are truly *yours*. I fail to see how I could do this, however, and remain realistic in my thinking. All our tastes have been influenced by the tastes of other people living and dead. If you judge contemporary poetry by the particular music of Shakespeare or the subtlety of Blake, your tastes have been definitely influenced by two human beings with whom you've never even conversed. If you evaluate a woman's beauty by the standards of Hollywood, without a doubt the star-makers have molded your thinking. If music appeals to you because it sounds like Benny Goodman or Johann Sebastian Bach, you're an influenced music lover. So? So, nothing. Except this is a fact as true of one member of the human race as another. And it is equally characteristic of us all, not always to agree where our tastes are concerned.

My brother Joe loves me dearly despite the fact that I have been a rabid admirer of the seemingly "way out" experimental writing of Gertrude Stein since I was fourteen. To him, this is near madness. To me, it makes marvelous sense. I love him dearly despite the fact that he is a hunter of squirrels and deer. This is strictly beyond me. But it is *his* taste and I respect it fully. I don't have to join him in his (to me) gruesome pastime, nor does he have to read Gertrude Stein's books. We recognize the fact that although we are the only two offspring of our parents, and have always been close, as people, we are "characters" of radically different tastes. I live in a house almost a hundred years old and wish it were still older. He and his wife have just bought a spanking new, ultra-contemporary ranch house and love it as much as I love my old three-story greystone. He loves the suburbs; I dislike them heartily and live as near Chicago's Loop as I can manage. Books, generally, bore my brother, Joe; I write them for a living. I wouldn't touch a rifle or a shotgun; he represents the Remington Firearms Company in the state of Ohio. We both love our work and we both love each other, and could any two people differ more? (I should add, we both *do* love my brother's boxer pup, Shah, and our wonderful Mother and the happy, happy memories of our Dad. There, outside of the fact that we share a knocked-out sense of humor, and dote on each other as human beings, the similarity stops.)

Is my taste superior to Joe's? No. Is his taste superior to mine? No. Just different. Definite in each case, because we are both definite people, but different.

How about you? Can you, *do* you still like the people (family or otherwise) whose taste differs wildly from yours? How about your feelings toward your parents when they plead or scream or order your favorite records silenced? Does this make them dull characters to you? Or have you matured enough to recognize that their taste is just different from yours? How do you feel about them when they go still farther "out" in your opinion, and turn on their own recordings of (to you) some "antiquity"? How would you feel toward me if I came to visit you, lugging my favorite recordings under my arm, and the sounds you heard when the first one dropped was a Vivaldi concerto? Then how about Miles Davis? Worse? Better? What's worse and what's better?

Perhaps the most important thing in this entire chapter on *Finding Out About Your Tastes* is this: we *can* learn to be objective where our tastes are concerned, and if we make

25

it in this area, we are well on our way to the kind of balanced objectivity that makes for a successful life.

You may hate the sound of classical music. Do you also shun the people you know who happen to love it? Do they shun you? You're both wrong if you do, both being immaturely subjective. It so happens that, to me, rock-and-roll is a sorry composite of the worst in the blues, southern and western folk music. Do you bore me because you disagree? Do I bore you because I think that way? Aren't we being ridiculous if this is the case?

Of course, *like* tastes form the strongest of human bonds. Last night a friend whom I have known for several years dressed me down for not having told her before that I am a devotee of Emily Dickinson's poetry. This would have given us one more bond, and a strong one.

Quite naturally, we enjoy the company of those who share our pet likes and even dislikes. (Dislikes we will tackle in the next chapter on *Prejudices*.) I have felt terribly alone through much of my Christian life simply because until recently I traveled so much and met so many people so fast, that I didn't have time to find many special friends who shared my most personal tastes in music, art, literature — even baseball. I am now convinced that this was good for me, because I was forced to realize that even people with so little in common as human beings could enjoy the one, everlasting, shining bond of the love of Jesus Christ. He bridges all tastes and prejudices! Now I have slowed down, am at home writing most of the time, and thoroughly delighted to have found a few other people who share not only my particular tastes in books, records and paintings, but my love for Jesus Christ as well. Up to now, when I was going so fast, we seldom took time to find out about each other as people; there were just too many meetings and arrangements and hurried dinners and whipped-up conversation and downright weariness.

I don't see as many people now, but I am learning more about the few I do see; and as I learn about them, I discover more and more about the God we follow. One of the things I am discovering about Him is that He does not love us according to our tastes. Even if you don't like gospel choruses,

He loves you just the same! And vice versa. You may hate the chorales of Bach and love the near-jazz of many gospel choruses. This is perfectly all right with God, *if* you don't dislike those of us who prefer a Bach chorale. You may love Mahler's *Song of the Earth* and despise the music of *Amazing Grace*. This is perfectly all right with God, *if* you don't likewise despise the people who prefer *Amazing Grace*. We all have our humanly-conceived notions of what is elevating. A Bach chorale elevates me endlessly. *Amazing Grace* gave my Dad the kind of lift no other music could have done. God is in Bach, God is in gospel choruses, God is in *Amazing Grace*. God is in the *Song of the Earth*, because God is everywhere, breaking through by many means to every available heart.

It is your *heart* which concerns Him first.

Your tastes are personal, and yours. The condition of your heart governs whether or not you inflict your tastes ruthlessly upon other people, or open yourself in love to the persons whose tastes may differ from yours.

This is a book about the tremendous potential *in you* for discovering your own answers along your own way. What a different world it would be if the people in it began to respect the differences in other people! More than that, what a difference it would make if we all began to respect, first of all, the *hearts* around us. God's heart is open to His entire beloved world. Jesus demonstrated that glorious fact as He hung on the cross with His heart (the very heart of God Himself) exposed, torn open, so that anyone could look inside.

Can we do less than open our hearts?

Yes, we can. We do, all of us, daily, do much, much less. We wrap ourselves tightly and snugly in our own little separate worlds of personal taste and look down our noses at those who are also wrapped in their own little separate worlds of personal taste, looking all the while down their noses at us. We don't have to have the same tastes in order to be open to one another, but because we are so ruled by our tastes — because we judge ourselves so finally by what is (to us) our own "good taste," we miss half the joy of sharing what *can* be shared with the other people whom God loves just as dearly as He loves us.

I have had some beautifully deep and meaningful evenings in the homes of people who would not have known Vivaldi, Stein or Dickinson, had I had the *bad* taste to bring them up. But we' were open to each other as people. Our hearts were open and we found love to share. We are all more comfortable when people neither look up to us nor down upon us, but accept us as fellow members of the human race.

And this brings us logically to the next point I must make — the need for exposure. God considers it all important, apparently. He *did* go to the extreme of exposing His own heart on the cross so that we *could* be drawn to Him by the magnetism of His love for us. How much do we really expose ourselves? Not only our hearts to other people, but how much do we really expose our tastes to possible development? Since we are so governed by what we consider good taste, or attractive or unattractive taste, wouldn't a direct path be opened to our hearts if we first of all decided to expose a few of our pet preferences? At one time I might have attempted to swing you to one or another of my personal tastes, arguing that, for this reason or that, I had the superior viewpoint. No more. I have merely become convinced that one of life's great keys is *openness* — willingness to be exposed to something new, that I will go no further than to urge you to try it.

For example, suppose you love football and think you hate baseball. This was true in reverse with me when I was in college. Because my Dad brought me up knowing and loving big league baseball, I peered down my nose at the "gauche" collegiate who waved a pennant and wore a "hideously huge" yellow mum to cheer on some muscular males who were senselessly tumbling all over themselves up and down a field knee-deep in mud. Then someone persuaded me to *expose* myself to football just once. But it had to be a real exposure. I was not to go full of rebellion because I preferred the Art Institute on a Saturday afternoon. I was not to go just because I had been so persuaded, and to sit there bored and scornful. I was to follow the plays as best I could with my limited knowledge of the game, and cheer for Northwestern (my school) when I could pick out a Northwestern player in the midst of the tumbling. In short, I was to participate — make it a genuine *exposure*.

Did it work? Of course it did. I still am not a rabid football addict; I still prefer baseball, but I do not despise you if you only endure the World Series and live for the day the football season gets under way. In fact, now I would choose a good book over either a football or a baseball game, but I'm delighted for *you*, whatever your preference may be. Can you be delighted for *me* if I am enjoying my book instead of huddling beside you under a blanket on the fifty-yard line?

My exposure to football did not make a fan of me, but it relieved me of the burden of having to feel superior to you who are fans. If you think you hate serious music, how about exposing yourself to just one good Beethoven symphony? Maybe you'd better start with Brahms. Or a simple, melodic Bach like *Jesu Joy of Man's Desiring*, or *Sheep May Safely Graze*. You won't have to turn into a 3B devotee, but it will do something for you in the maturity department. Like me at that football game, you'll have to stop fidgeting, though. Drop your rebellion. Don't sit there and think, "Me dig this stuff? Genie Price and the birds can have it! Not me." That's not the way of real exposure.

How do you know you don't like Shakespeare or Emily Dickinson? Have you ever read either of them when you didn't have to in order to get through a course? How do you know you don't like even the sound of church music? Have you ever listened to it with your heart? How do you know you don't like to read the Bible? Ever read it — just for yourself? Of course, there are passages in it you may not fully understand, but have you ever really exposed your mind and your heart to some of the simple words of Jesus? This is quite an experience, providing you can drop your self-consciousness, the rebellions you've come to use as excuses, and really open yourself to what you read.

Exposure to new, creative, unfamiliar experiences is one of life's great excitements. I hate to see you miss it. This is not an attempt to convert you from your taste to mine. This is a dare! I dare you to give yourself a chance to *add* to your tastes, instead of clinging for dear life to those you have. Maybe Mom has a point. Dad even. Who knows? This much I know: God has a great deal more for us here in this fabulous world than we permit ourselves to discover. Just because something is familiar does not mean it is *best*. It may be — but with Him, there is always more and still more to find out.

A wise high school senior said to me not long ago, "Nope, no going steady for me. My taste in women changes too fast! My taste changes too fast — period. Last month I was still making fancy model cars. My girl raved about them, so I thought she was great. Now, she's still pulling the same old stuff and I'm interested in something else."

Your tastes will change too. Not all of them, perhaps, but don't let yourself get stuck with people or things you may outgrow. Your taste in music may change, but there will always be music to love. Why not expose yourself to its wide and lofty varieties *now* and find out for yourself what you really like?

Your tastes in books may change, but there will always be books to love. Don't limit yourself to one kind of books now. Experiment.

God is the great Experimenter . . . "In the beginning God . . ." One thing sure to which you can tie forever — His interest in you and your taste. Get personally acquainted with Him. His taste is flawless and you can experiment forever under His control. "In Him you are complete." In Him you can discover your *best* you.

5 Finding Out About Your Prejudices

If you are a faddist, without realizing it you can acquire a whole batch of new *prejudices*. Prejudice means pre-judging — drawing your own conclusions after weighing only one side of the issue. Invariably a prejudice implies lopsidedness, lack of fairness. How does following a fad lead to prejudice? Here's an illustration: One Christmas I bought my nephew a good-looking black leather jacket. When he opened it, he tried to be polite, but his prejudice was too strong! "Boy, Aunt Gene, that's great, but you don't think I'd be caught dead in this thing, do you?" His point? Only a certain kind of rebel wore black leather jackets — the "delinquents," as he called them. If I had used my head five seconds, I'd have realized this. The "fad" among the tough-guy motorcycle crowd was black leather jackets. My nephew was caught on the reverse side of a fad, but his prejudice bloomed anyway. Mother and I both made a botch of our Christmas shopping simply because we hadn't been around high-schoolers enough to keep up on the latest fads. She had bought several handsome pairs of trousers for him. They had to go back to the store, too. "What would the other guys I know think about me with these big, bloomy pants?" The fad was trousers so tight they all but had to be reseamed each morning! And my otherwise easy-going nephew really got upset at the thought that someone might think he didn't know any better than to wear trousers in which he could actually bend over. "I can't stand these floppy guys — they're creeps."

Prejudice because of a fad.

Are fads wrong? Not necessarily, but they are temporary. Perhaps they do no real damage, at least most of them, *until* they begin to sew the seeds of prejudice. Mother and I gladly exchanged my nephew's jacket and trousers for more acceptable gifts. That was unimportant. The important thing was that he seemed unable to follow the fad without being prejudiced against those who did not follow it, or could not. Some young people just can't afford to be faddish. Do they deserve your prejudice?

Fads leading to prejudices, unfortunately, are not limited

to high-schoolers or college students and their peculiarities in dress. They invade even the ranks of Christendom among adults. Any time you find a group moving *against* another group, you will find prejudice, and frequently it has come into being as a consequence of what could be called a fad. This mass approval or disapproval is often "backed up by Scripture" (isolated, of course), and it is frequently called "contending for the faith." But is it? Isn't it often just contention? And doesn't it gain momentum because it is the opinion of the herd? Has anyone really thought it through?

"I don't think my roommate's a Christian at all," one college girl wrote, "because she wears make-up and goes to dances. Oh, she prays every night and reads her Bible, but every time I see her on her knees I feel like jerking her up — it seems like blasphemy to me!"

Prejudice? All the way, as I see it.

According to the Bible, faith in Jesus Christ makes a human being a Christian. This girl had been prejudiced through the thoughtless adults in her church, and she was going to contend for the prejudice or else. When I asked her to explain her attitude, she only grew more vehement. She had not thought it through at all. If you sincerely believe a Christian should not wear make-up or read a certain version of the Bible, this is your prerogative. All I am asking is that you think through your reasons first. Christians are not all at the same place in what they see to be right and wrong. Are we not being truly un-Christian when we decide *for* them to the extent that our hearts flare *against* them?

"Yes, he says he's a Christian," a well-known Christian leader remarked, "but I don't think much of his Christianity — he reads those modern translations of the Bible!"

Prejudice? Indeed it is. Prejudice to the extent of playing God in another man's life. But if we face it honestly, no human being can really play God. None of us can see that clearly. None of us can be that impartial. None of us can love enough. Only God can be God, and He never *pre*judges. He alone has all the facts at hand, and He alone can sort them out and draw perfectly accurate conclusions.

We like to temper or soften our prejudices by calling them preferences. This is just not honest. Preferences are tastes. Prejudices are biased. Preferences and tastes show leanings *toward.* Prejudices show leanings *against* or *away from.*

What about you? Are you prejudiced? Is there some area in which you just can't be budged away from your opinion? If so, this may be good. But it also may be the sign of a whole flock of deep-seated prejudices. Think it through. Does it have to do with your background? Your talents? Your taste? If the kind of music you like to hear hour in and hour out sounds like so much noise to me, does this turn you against me? It would have turned me against you once, before I began to think through my opinions — from your viewpoint as well as mine.

"Those kids can't be worth much or they wouldn't like that hideous stuff they call music!" Spoken like a spoiled, thoughtless brat, by the father of a college freshman who had brought a few of her friends in for cokes after ice-skating one night. This (to me) spoiled-brat father happened to be the president of the college, no less! I was speaking on the campus and was a guest in the president's home. We are not discussing the young people's taste in music here. The father is the gentleman in question now. If he had been on his feet addressing the student body in chapel, he would have thought it through. *All* young people — all people, for that matter, are of inestimable worth to God, regardless of their taste in music! The man spoke out of prejudice and emotion. He was embarrassed for me to know his daughter had what to him was deplorable taste. True, the young people lacked courtesy; one hour might have been long enough, what with other older people in the house. But there is a much better way than the way Papa used that night. He became so enraged that he ordered the young people to leave and instructed his daughter, "that bunch is never to set foot in this house again."

Was he prejudiced? I think so, yes. It sometimes requires a long, long time, but adults have the obligation to elevate your tastes, not to condemn you for them.

Prejudice always *excludes.*

Love always *includes.*

What does this really mean? Does it mean that you are to be lax and stupidly inclusive in your choice of friends, recreation, books and ideas? Of course not. Is God stupid? And is there a more *inclusive* love in existence than the love of God? Did God die with His arms stretched out toward the whole world, as the Bible says in John 3:16, or is this a mistake?

Human love, even at its best, is exclusive. We tend to stay inside our own little safety areas, where people think the way we think, do the things we do, and don't do the things we don't do. We snuggle inside our own familiar, small nests politically, socially and religiously. The poor man was out of office before I could bring myself to pray for Harry Truman when he was President. He was not another Jefferson in my opinion, but actually, once I began to think it through, the main thing I had against him was his politics! Relax, my good Democrat friends. I am now, first of all, a Christian. At the time I am writing this book, we have a Democratic President, whom I admire very much. God has shown me the superficiality of my once *exclusive* political prejudices. "Thanks be to God," I now do not have to agree totally with a man in order to respect him as a fellow human being and a statesman. I now do not have to agree totally with anyone, in order to love, to be concerned about, to care for him.

Like you, perhaps, many of my prejudices have been — and still are — quite dear to me. They become familiar and comfortable, and supply us with quick, easy answers. Letting them go is not a simple matter, and it is often painful. We feel somewhat bereft. It may necessitate some study, some diligent thinking, and almost always it is humiliating to see ourselves as having been so ignominiously superficial for so many years. But once we begin to examine our prejudices in the Presence of One who "so loved the world," we find ourselves unable not to strip them off, one by one. Actually, after a while it ceases to be a one-by-one process, and becomes a totally new attitude of heart.

Before my Father went to be with the Lord a few years ago, he and I had a moment of truth before God one night, driving home in his car, which I shall never forget. I was born in a border-line Southern state — West Virginia. To insure a lack of race prejudice in my brother and me, our parents had taught us well that the color of a man's skin made no difference whatever in his human worth. As a result, being more of an extremist than my brother, I went overboard and ended up with a genuine, bona-fide prejudice against white people who held prejudice against Negroes. For three or four years after my conversion to Jesus Christ, every time I went into the deep South to speak, Billy Holiday's husky voice singing *Strange Fruit*, the lynching song, haunted my every waking hour! I seemed to hear it even above the hymns in the churches where I spoke. I was confiding this problem to my Dad that night in his car, as we drove home. This caused him to launch on a story of a church woman who had blocked a Negro family from joining a church in West Virginia. For about ten minutes we both sat there in the front seat of the car and tossed around our self-righteousness and prejudice and condemnation of this poor segregationist sister. Finally, God got in a word to us both. With a thud our spiritual egos crashed at the realization that we were as guilty as she! We were as prejudiced against her "and her kind" as she was against the Negro family. We both saw it, asked forgiveness, laughed in relief — and I have been like a bird out of a cage on every trip south of the Mason-Dixon line ever since!

With all of me I am opposed to race segregation, but my heart is no longer locked and my fists are not up against those who hold to it.

Prejudice is a pronounced sign of immaturity. Perhaps we could say that prejudice is normal in children. They are simply not mentally developed enough to think it through. It is true, of course, that children acquire most of their basic prejudices from adults. Perhaps you have heard the true story of the little fellow whose mother asked if his new playmate, George, was a Negro. "What does that mean?" the boy questioned. "Well, the ladies tell me you are playing with a little colored boy, dear. Is George's skin black?" The boy thought a minute and said, "I don't know, Mommie. I'll look tomorrow."

The foregoing is an example of the kind of prejudice that is planted in the child's formative mind. There is another kind of prejudice, however, which I believe to be normal with youngsters, and which is relatively harmless as long as they are young. The damage results when they keep this same kind of closed mind as adults. For example, when I was a child, I firmly believed that my daddy was the *only* really skillful dentist in the whole city of Charleston, West Virginia. My uncle practiced with him in the same suite of offices, but this was beside the point. I don't think I dwelt on him at all, one way or another. Of one thing only was I sure: Daddy was the best! So deeply did I believe this that I well remember the day I rushed to the telephone in the principal's office at school, to call my mother so she could do something to stop my school chum's mother from going to Dr. So-and-So for an extraction. I was dead sure the woman might even die if anyone but my father performed the operation.

I know some Christians who are almost this extreme where their particular denomination is concerned. I also know some parents who feel this way about their children. My conviction about my father's skill was a downright belief. When Mother explained the situation, I let down the barriers and allowed a few of my father's professional colleagues into the fold. A *belief* is quite different from a *prejudice*, providing we hold the belief after careful thought and study. A genuine belief never motivates us in the negative. The Communist countries have allowed their beliefs to turn into prejudices against the free world. The free world can be guilty of the same thing. We hate their dogma, but we must not hate the people who hold it. Not if we are true followers of the One who opened His arms from the beginning, to the whole world.

A good way to check ourselves for prejudices and/or beliefs is this: What happens to your blood pressure? What happens to your disposition? When your dearest theories are challenged or knocked down, do you flare up? Do you grow angry and want to hit back? Do you want to defend yourself? Do you want to knock down the other fellow's opinions? If you have come to a definite conclusion *before* you have weighed the evidence on both sides, before you have stepped over into the other fellow's shoes for even a moment, then you can be fairly sure that you are *pre*-judging. You have ended up with a prejudice. You are not acting on what you have thought through, because you have not used your mind at all. You have formed your conclusion on your *emotions*. Therefore, it is quite natural that when your conclusion is challenged, your emotions flare. If you have thought it through carefully, and are sure of your conviction, your emotions are beside the point. Furthermore, you are then so certain, that your security is in no way challenged.

The "fighters" in Christendom always strike me as being basically afraid someone is going to prove them wrong. If a man or a woman is sure, from having looked objectively at both sides of the problem, he is also secure. Only then can we discuss and not be tempted to flare up or even to argue.

There is a whole world full of people out there, beyond your personal boundaries, who not only need your understanding, they may need your light. Don't be afraid of them and, above all, don't pre-judge them. The Father has given all judgment into the hands of Jesus Christ. And He is incapable of prejudice.

6 *Finding Out About God*

It is utterly true that God is incapable of prejudice, but do you think many people have ever really thought about this? If one took time to think through the characteristics of God demonstrated plainly by Jesus on His cross, it would seem to me to be impossible to cringe before Him as so many people do.

In no way do I mean to imply that He is a "grandmother of the lace-cap variety" God, who encourages us to get by with as much as possible. There is nothing in the nature of the One who hung on the cross that leads to pampering. He is a holy God, and with all the energy of His God-heart, He did and still does battle with anything that harms His loved ones. But He does not pre-judge. He cannot, because He *is* understanding. Prejudice always carries with it the lack of understanding. Prejudice propels one toward harm. God's understanding propels one toward redemption, re-creation.

I have written an entire book (*Strictly Personal*) on the *adventure of discovering what God is really like*. Even so, I anticipate difficulty in confining myself to a single chapter here on the same subject. It is an always opening subject, an always continuing adventure, an eternal discovery. For over fourteen years now, this discovery has occupied my attention. It would seem perfectly logical to me to find out that we will go through all eternity still discovering new things about this God we worship. "I am the beginning and the end," Jesus said. If this is true, how could there be an end to His nature? This, and this alone, stimulates me toward heaven.

Whatever else of wonder will be there, the bright, central wonder of heaven will *have* to be God Himself. We are with Him now, if we are His followers, but here we have the disadvantage of this "fussy veil" of earthly life. There we will be with Him without barriers of any kind. There we will see Him as we are unable to see Him now. There we will be exposed, in our freed inner-selves, to His inner-self, and the exposure can only lead us on to more and more discovery. We will find Him irresistible. We will find Him full of joy and love and interest. We will find Him stimulating us in what will then be a perfectly natural way, toward endless discovery. There, goals will be beside the point. He will fill our *now*, and *now* will be eternal; boredom, strain and the need for discipline will be forgotten. We will be completely absorbed with God Himself.

To me, the beginning of eternal life on this earth is as simple as the beginning of one's personal interest in the very nature of God. The instant I opened my heart to faith in His existence, my interest in His nature leaped into being. In the years since, I have not tired once of *considering* God in Jesus Christ — considering His intentions toward us, His children, and toward the entire human race. Considering His unlimited love, His unlimited wisdom, His unlimited desire to be one with us. Sometimes I sit for a long time, just considering His energy — the energy of God paling the energy we have learned to release atomically from the sun, paling all the forces of the combined energies of all the universes man can locate or imagine. If I only considered this energy, however, and did not know the nature of the heart that motivates it, I would tremble with terror.

I do know that Heart, though, and so can anyone know it. Anyone can know God because anyone can know Jesus.

Do you wish it were more complicated? Is yours the type of mind which refuses to settle for simplicity? Does simplicity insult your intelligence? I understand this, if it's true of you. And you're not alone. But neither are you God. This is no insult to you. This fact is not intended to belittle you. It is simply a fact. And the truly intelligent mind recognizes the necessity to accept facts and proceed from there. The difference between you and God is not a difference of *degree*, it is a difference of *kind*. Only the unrealistic man insists upon his own supremacy. Many do insist upon it, but this really complicates matters. And it *is* utterly unrealistic and unworkable.

Suppose for a moment that man could be supreme and final in himself. Just who is this "man"? Is it mankind in general? If so, look at the world he has governed for all these centuries. Is it only the good man, or only the good in man that is supreme? Is it only man's potential? The questions grow progressively vague, don't they?

Finally, they dwindle out.

But if we begin with one truly Supreme Being — God — then we have a starting place. Then we as human beings no longer need to try to "tune ourselves" to each other. We are in possession of a totally freeing Absolute. Just as the members of a symphony orchestra tune their separate instruments to a master note, so we can be tuned to God, our Master. If He created the entire human race in the beginning, surely His way is the way of harmony. Surely He knows how to return us to the harmony He intended us to enjoy. The returning is gigantic, but it *is* simple.

I have traveled the roads of philosophy, science, logic, and many of the other religions. I revel now in the fresh air of the simplicity and intelligence of loving God.

This chapter is not, however, an attempt to persuade you that God *is*. It is predicated, as the Bible is predicated, on the fact of His being. We are interested in discovering — finding out for ourselves — what God is really like.

I am a Christian. If you are, too, then you have a continuing and direct way of discovering God's true nature for yourself. Any Christian has. Christianity holds that God Himself, in the Person of Jesus Christ, broke into human history so that anyone — no matter what his background or education or lack of it — can discover God personally. Adherents of the other religions may understandably think us bigots. This is simply not true. If we are *thinking* followers of the One who allowed the beings He created to nail Him to a criminal's cross, we simply cannot feel superior for believing that God and Jesus Christ are one. This knowledge, planted in the human heart by the Holy Spirit of the Crucified, is the only sure way to true humility. Christians who argue their faith have missed the dynamic of it. They have not followed Him in the most plainly spoken direction He gave us when He was on earth: "Learn of Me, for I am meek and lowly in heart." We give lip service to His words, but we have not really *learned* of Him if there is a single streak of arrogance staining our faith!

If we have discovered anything of the true nature of the God-Man, we not only do not argue, we *cannot*. We will want to learn to *communicate* our faith — to *witness*, but never argumentatively. It has been said, and truly, that we cannot sit in the judge's seat and the witness box at the same time.

Granted that you have learned enough of the true character of God so that you no longer feel "superior" or seek to win a point for "your side," have you learned enough about Him to be able to communicate His love in your Christian witness? A Christian witness is not merely a statement of what you believe. It is not merely an expression of your own experience. Jesus said we were to be witnesses *unto Him.*

How can we communicate truth about Someone whom we do not know well personally? It is perfectly possible to know a great deal *about* someone, without knowing that person yourself. Depending upon your political beliefs, or the section of the country where you happen to live, your "witness" to the President of the United States could vary so much from mine that someone who knew nothing about him might not know we spoke of the same man! Do you "witness" to Christ this way? Are you limited by your background? Your minister's point of view? The clichés or lack of them which appeal to you? I am not speaking of methods of witnessing now; I am speaking of your knowledge of the One about whom you witness.

Some Christians have such a distorted concept of God, I feel it might be best if they just kept still most of the time.

"I have a wonderful Christian mother," a college sophomore wrote to me not long ago. "She lives in fear and trembling of the God of Israel and was always so strict on me that I live in fear of Him, too. Surely no one could say my mother is not a consecrated woman, but the God she taught me to revere does not sound like the God you write about in your book, *Strictly Personal.* Mother says I shouldn't be filling my mind with things like you write. If she knew I had written to you, she would be furious. I try so hard not to do anything that would displease Him, but now that I am in college and away from Mother, I am more and more nervous for fear I don't really know Him well enough to be sure I am not displeasing to the Lord."

I could weep over this young man. Yes, it was a young man, believe it or not. Usually one thinks of a daughter's having fallen so utterly under Mama's spell. Not this time. I could tell this young man that he was absolutely right in thinking he did not know the Lord well enough. With all his heart he had followed his *mother's God*. Perhaps more accurately, he had followed his *mother*. I don't know his mother's God either, and sincere though I believe the woman to be, I don't think I'd care to know Him. "The God of Israel" revealed His *true* nature once and for all, so that anyone could comprehend it, the day the young Man hung on His cross with His arms stretched out to the whole world. Until we know the God who was reconciling (harmonizing) the whole world to Himself in Jesus Christ, we simply do not have a very clear picture of the Deity. "If you have known Me, you have known the Father," Jesus said. Was He wrong? "I and the Father are one." Could they be one and contradict one another? Would the Holy Spirit of the same God whom Jesus came to reveal point anyone to a distorted image of the Father? Would the members of the Godhead disagree with one another? Would the Father contradict the Son? Or the Son the Father? Would the Holy Spirit contradict either? Can God disagree with Himself? No.

So then, if the Bible is correct when it tells us that the Spirit will make clear the things of God to us, how is it that this same Spirit of the same God who exposed His heart on Calvary could give such widely varying images of Himself to His poor, struggling earthlings? He would not do this, of course. He does not do it.

God paid a visit to this earth for one basic reason: He wanted each of us, once and for all, to find out what He is really like! In order to clarify our misunderstandings, Jesus said over and over: "You have heard it said of olden times . . . but *I* say unto you!" It is as though He was reaching toward every human heart, with every ounce of His enormous energy, in an all-out divine effort to get us to look at Him! To correct our distorted concepts. It is as though He cried: "Look at Me . . . learn about Me . . . find out what I am really like and then you will know all you need to know about the Father!"

A continuing, direct look at God, as He showed Himself to be in Christ, *draws* us to willing, love-filled obedience. There is nothing in the heart that broke on the cross which fills me with negative, unhealthy, cringing fear. *God's se-*

verest punishment is the punishment of increased love in the ugly face of our disobedience. Even as they laughed at His agony on the cross, Jesus prayed for them. The worse they treated Him, the more love He seemed to pour down upon them! He knows, because He is God that nothing will break the spell of sin over the human heart except the full application of divine love, the "love that will *not* let us go." Not the love that terrorizes us into *being afraid* to go.

"I, if I be lifted up . . . will *draw* all men unto Me."

It is not God's way to tell a struggling human being that he is to believe simply because God is God. He will never ask you to accept your particular heartache or grief, just because He is God ordering you to do it. He longs for us to know for ourselves what He is really like. He, more than anyone else, knows that the human heart — yours or mine — *can* trust Him in the deep, dark places *until* that human heart knows Him as He *is*. I firmly believe God prefers honest rebellion to the whipped-dog acquiescence of a human being just because it is supposed to be the religious thing to do.

Now that Jesus has come, no one ever again has to wonder about Him. He is discoverable to everyone. Of course, no human mind or heart could contain the knowledge of the whole of God, but with all my being I know that I can learn all I need to learn of His intentions, His heart, His ways, through knowing Jesus Christ personally. "He has made Him known." My puzzling can come to an end, my knowing can begin. I can stop wondering *about* God and begin to wonder *at* Him.

All that could be contained of God in a human being came to dwell among us when Jesus was born. He Himself was God in the flesh. He died for love of us, but He is alive now and still among us through the very real Person of His Spirit. We do not follow a phantom, but a living Person who invites us hourly to face Him with our doubts, our questions, our uncertainties. "Come unto Me . . . learn of Me."

Discover God for yourself in Christ. Give Him your close attention, your scrutiny, ask Him your questions. Find out for yourself what He is really like.

After all, He is the only Person alive in the world who can bear complete inspection, and He lovingly invites it.

7 *Finding Out What You Really Believe*

Here I have no intention, in fact, see no need for us to enter the scarred arena where so-called liberalism and conservatism do battle with each other. Both movements long have been, and still are under attack, from each other and those in between. Paul Tillich once pointed out that whenever a movement is under attack, it tends to narrow itself. It ducks behind what it fervently hopes is an impenetrable fortress and does battle, not only with its adversaries from outside, but with what it believes to be subversives within. I have been labeled a liberal by ultra-conservatives and a conservative by ultra-liberals.

If my opinion matters, I am a Christian who believes with all my heart that Jesus Christ *was* God in the flesh, and that because of my belief in *Him* as my Saviour, my life has been returned to harmony with the Creator, God. I believe God and Jesus Christ are one and the same — the great Creator *did* become my Saviour.

We will not involve ourselves in the marginal issues which split Christendom into its often confusing dogmas and schisms. We are concerned only with finding out what *you* really believe.

I remember vividly one night in the year 1949, when the friend who led me to a living faith in Jesus Christ sat talking about what she really believed. I remember so vividly because, although she expressed herself well, I shut her off abruptly when she said she believed that Jesus Christ died on a cross to redeem the world from sin. "Cut that stuff," I snapped. "I want to know what *you* really believe about this God you say you follow! What does He have to do with *you*, day by day? How does your life as a Christian really differ from mine? What difference does it make in the tight places?"

Wisely, she said no more that night about her actual theological beliefs and spoke only of Jesus Christ. Theological beliefs are important, make no mistake about it. I used to pride myself on the fact that I was no theologian. From platform after platform, I announced the fact — implying
44

somehow, that this made me special. I didn't consciously think so, but in the first days of my new life with God, I quite naturally (as does almost every new Christian) felt I was the possessor of some particularly potent insight. What was really happening, as I see it now in retrospect, was this: The Holy Spirit was doing just what Jesus said He would do for anyone. He was teaching me as fast as I was teachable. Being teachable merely means we have recognized our deep need and are open to having that need met by God. He was meeting my need, and I was literally whirling with all the light that was coming to me so suddenly. I felt "special," perhaps, because I had never known this to happen to anyone before. My life as an adult had not been spent among people who had experienced the direct effects of His cross in their lives. My conversion was a whole new world to me in every way. My mother was a believer, but she had met Him before I was born. I remember "revival" meetings in our church when I was a child, but what I remember appealed not at all to me as an adult. Until the very day of my conversion, I had not been inside a church of any kind in eighteen years. All churches were one long, pink blur to me, and October 2, 1949, when I attended the morning worship service at Calvary Episcopal Church in New York City, I went only to please my friend who had been so patient with me.

When Holy Communion was offered to all who cared to participate, I *tried* to take part with the same motive of pleasing her. I was halfway down the sloping church aisle toward the altar, where Dr. Samuel Shoemaker stood waiting to serve the Lord's Supper, when the first bolt of real insight concerning my *un*belief struck me. I could not join the others at that altar. Instead, I turned and ran from the church, not even aware that the people might be watching me.

Why was I unable to go through with communion? My regard for my kind friend enabled me to get up on a Sunday morning and dress — even to the hated hat — in order to attend church. Why was I suddenly unable to go through with one more gesture? Quite simply, I see now that it was at that moment that I recognized the distance between God and me! Polite gestures could not bridge the gap. Regard for my friend, or even the regard I had by then for her belief, could not bridge it. Something had to be done. And it was. That afternoon in my hotel room I linked my life with the life of Jesus Christ. By His Spirit, *I began to believe for myself.*

This is the moment certain Christians express as being "saved." I hated the word then, but I was saved just the same. God was such a stranger to me, I don't even remember praying. But I was in communion with Him. We made an eternal transaction with each other. Perhaps, if I am theologically correct, I should say that He verified what He had already done for me. The active part of the transaction was probably mine. Whatever is "correct" to say, we exchanged lives. I couldn't handle mine any longer, and I suddenly knew that He *could* handle it. I needed His life desperately, and He gave it to me, as He will give it to anyone who is open to it. For the first time in my thirty-three years, I consciously cooperated with God's will.

Since then, He has never been an ogre with an indomitable will to which I must bend my neck. In almost every area of my life I had to submit to deep change. But He has always managed to bring about my ultimate obedience — not by "lording" it over me, but by *being* the Lord of my heart. He is the Lord of my heart because of what I have learned about His heart.

If you had asked me that day, or the day after, or even weeks after, I probably could not have explained to you in language satisfactory to the orthodox doctrine-watcher what had happened to me — what I really believed *about* Him. But I haven't met anyone who doubted that I *believed* Him. One Chicago Christian leader said of me several years after my conversion, as he introduced me on a radio broadcast: "I met Genie Price soon after her conversion. I can honestly say I had never met anyone who knew *less* about what had happened to her, but I had also never met anyone about whom I was more certain something *had* happened!"

I made all sorts of almost unpardonable *faux pas* when I talked to long-time Christians. I used the word *fundamentalist* when I meant *liberal* and smiled in innocent (or ignorant) agreement with the wrong people, totally mixed up as to their meaning of such phrases as "eternal security" and other theological terms. When Mr. Harry Saulnier, superintendent of the Pacific Garden Mission, whose radio series, *Unshackled*, I was writing and directing, asked if a certain actor we employed was *separated*, I glibly replied: "Oh no — he's one of the most happily married men I know!"

The words, the man-invented language of the Kingdom, I did not know; but I knew the King, and with all my heart I believed in *Him*.

Now, what does it really mean to believe in Christ? Have you ever thought about that? What does it mean to *you?* I am not asking what words you use when you speak publicly in His behalf, or give what is known as a "testimony." What does it mean in your daily life that you believe in Jesus Christ as God, and as the Lord of your hours and days and years? Remember now, we are not delving into theological explanations of this doctrine or that. We are thinking solely about *what you really believe.*

Perhaps you are thinking about the fact that now that your faith is in Him, you will go to heaven instead of to that place Dante wrote about so realistically. This, too, is not the main point here. I expect to spend eternity in His Presence, too, but what about today?

"My belief in Christ shows up most in my life because of the things I don't do that other students do." This statement, believe it or not, was made by the president of the small, fairly uninteresting Christian group on a large university campus. Do you wonder that the group was small? And uninteresting? What's interesting about what you *don't* do? The Moslems stick to their prohibitions much more religiously than most Christians. Jesus didn't say, "Your don'ts, if they be lifted up, will draw all men unto Me." He said, "*I*, if *I* be lifted up . . ."

How do people so confuse His meaning? How do even His followers manage to get the emphasis on the marginal issues, when He Himself is the attraction? Foolish question number 5000! We won't even try to answer it, except to say that it must be because they don't think it through.

In her excellent little book, *The Years That Count*, my friend Rosalind Rinker tells a gem of a story which actually occurred during the years in which she worked as a staff counselor for Inter-Varsity Christian Fellowship on secular campuses in the western part of the United States. One year at the beginning of the fall term a Christian girl exclaimed: "Ros, I've witnessed to every girl in my wing of the dorm!" Knowing that meant about fifty or more girls, Ros asked how she managed it so quickly.

"Well, we were all together one night when someone asked me if I'd take a blind date for a dance. I got their attention and simply made an announcement to the whole gang. I said it would be useless for anyone else to try to fix me up for a date to a dance, because I didn't dance. Also, no point in offering me a cigarette, because I didn't smoke, nor wear make-up, nor go to movies, etc., etc." Then the young lady remembered to add, "I'm a Christian."

Ros looked her in the eye and grinned. "Now I suppose they all want to be just like you, don't they?"

When we witness to Jesus Christ, it should have some connection at least with what we really *believe*. This girl had not thought it through. She was getting what to her was a nasty job off her hands in the quickest possible way.

Once more, we are not dealing with negatives in this book. Jesus came that we might have life and have it more abundantly. I linked my life with His *not* to be rid of my pleasures (I wasn't that crazy!); I entered into the eternal relationship with Him because *He drew me to Himself*.

Christianity *is* Jesus Christ, not a batch of rules. There is nothing *static* about belonging to Him. Or there should not be. There need not be. He is always in motion toward us in love, and what people twist into prohibitions and "don'ts" started out to be — or are, in reality — merely our loving responses to His love toward us. If you really love someone, and if you really believe in that person's inner-self and intentions toward you, you don't go about hurting him, do you? God is not a policeman lengthening our police records in His big black book with every misdemeanor, in righteous patience waiting for the day when He can get even with us! He is our Father who loves us with a love so wide we can't even comprehend it, and when we do anything that harms us, we hurt Him.

What does it really mean to believe in Christ? How does it affect you when the going is rough? When your life is especially full of joy? Or success? Or failure? Real faith, real belief in God means that we *act* on what we *know* of Him. Remember, we can know Him better with every passing day. There is one Book you can never drain dry, and that's the Bible. With every reading you can acquire more and more personal knowledge of the nature of God. With every new experience lived out with Him, your knowledge can increase. Ask the Holy Spirit to make it clear to you how deeply and eternally God loves every person in the whole wide world, and watch this new realization increase your own understanding and belief in Him. The whole thing takes on a progressive rhythm: The more you learn of Him, the more your belief in Him is strengthened, increased, made usable.

Genuine belief in God means we literally commit ourselves to acting in the tight places as though He *is* exactly who He claims to be. We *find out for ourselves* about Him firsthand, and then we go His way. And as we do this year after year, we discover to our great, glad amazement that more and more His way seems to be our way. The relationship grows more and more natural, as God becomes more and more familiar. The strain decreases as our knowledge of Him increases. Then one day, we find — not that we are sprouting wings, or wearing sparkling halos at just the perfect angle — but that it has been a long, long time since we have even considered acting independently of Him. We do not discover ourselves to be rigid ascetics, flailing ourselves into submission to a fearsome God. We truly discover our *selves* — our real selves — and find them at home and interested and actively loyal to a loving Father.

Real belief, as I see it, is not merely keeping score on our obediences and stacking up guilt over our disobediences. *Real belief is love in motion* — confidence in the fact that His love is always in motion toward us, in our behalf, *and* increased joy in the motion of our own love responses to Him. Things do not need to be going magnificently well for us to experience this kind of creative living with God. It can show itself at its shiniest and most convincing best when our hearts are breaking for any of the reasons any human heart may break. What do you really believe?

Is it your own belief, born of those moments of conscious communion between you and God? Or is it your parents' belief, modified into some sort of almost-working arrangement for you? If you are a Christian, are you a first-hander? If not, could this be the reason so many of your friends seem uninterested in this God to whom you say you belong? It is informative to read the biography of a great person, written by an author who knew him well; but what a difference if you could have known that great person yourself. I can become absorbed for hours reading what someone else has written about Thomas Jefferson, but I have stood on the wide portico of his home at Monticello and longed painfully for just five minutes of face-to-face conversation with the great man. I can walk through his beautiful gardens now, and know that they look much the same as when he walked there, but something is missing for me — Mr. Jefferson himself is not there. He will never be there again; he is dead. You and I can become devoteés of his life and his memory, but we cannot get in touch with *him*. We must always be second-handers where the man from Monticello is concerned. This is not true of God. No one needs to be a second-hander with Him. He is alive. He got up and walked out of His tomb. He is with us and in us now, in Person, by His Spirit.

Is your belief your own? Are you in touch with Him personally? If so, are you allowing Him to come through to you as only He knows how to do? Or are you keeping Him a bit at arm's length because something in your religious background, or some well-meaning but confused person has given you the erroneous idea that He is remote from the human race? Perhaps you are keeping Him at arm's length because you are afraid He will ask something of you which will make you unhappy. This God we worship is not unknowable! Anyone can discover what He is really like, so why take a chance on missing His best for you just because you are vague about His real nature? Why suspect God of the worst, when He went to such great length to give you His best?

Find out what you really believe about Him in the areas where it concerns you most, and then be adventuresome enough to begin right now to act on it! It may be a small knowledge at the start, but with Him everything grows.

8 *Finding Out How to Be With God*

One of the last things most of us seem to discover is that there is only one way to be with God, and that is to be *yourself*. He knows everything there is to know about you anyway, so why do so many Christians assume a pious sounding tone of voice, a manner of speaking which they never use otherwise, and a long, studiously serious countenance when they talk to the One who not only created them in the first place, but who never for one minute allows them to slip His mind?

What do I mean by being with God? Everything. But perhaps we should look seriously at the matter of actual prayer first. Certainly this is concentrated *being* with Him. If we love someone dearly and know that person has a difficult ordeal ahead, or if two lovers face a long separation, it is perfectly natural to say, "I'll be with you." This is not merely lover-talk, or words strung together to comfort a friend in trouble. We mean it. And we do have a way, because we are creatures of spirit, to "be with" someone, even though miles and seemingly endless time may stretch between us. In one sense, surely, we are always with God. Without a doubt, He is always with us!

What about you and God when you pray? Do you really talk to each other? Do you converse? Or is it a one-sided tirade in which you do all the talking? If you haven't read Rosalind Rinker's book called *Prayer — Conversing With God*, don't waste any more time. Many of you will have read it, because young people particularly are usually honest enough to admit that the typical prayer meeting bores them. She goes right to the heart of this and gives you an interesting, logical, provocative way out of that boredom. I urge you to read her book; but for our purposes here, let's really think briefly through this matter of prayer.

Is it dull to you? Is it foreign?

Does your whole personality change when you begin to talk to God? If so, this is all right with Him — He knows you exactly as you are, anyway. The loss is on your side. You are probably imitating some adults whom you've heard pray in a certain fashion, and you are not being entirely *you*. You are not being insincere, but without realizing it, you are perhaps being false. In no way am I recommending lack of reverence. We need to think this through, too. Is being natural, being your real self, irreverent? Of course not. Many Christians who share a personal, intimate experience with God tend to feel somewhat superior to the Christian who makes use of ritual and liturgy. But if we are honest, if we are really thinking, what is the basic difference? How personal and how intimate is your relationship with Him? If you constantly fall back on the usual handful of prayer clichés which you have heard dozens of people use for years, is this much different from reading prayers? Make it a point to listen the next time you participate in a prayer meeting. This isn't being sacrilegious. This is just thinking. Not long ago I took part in a prayer time before one of my speaking engagements. Most likely the others would have been shocked if they knew I was counting how many of the well-meaning, but (to me) unalert people asked God to be with us! "Oh, Lord, we ask You to be with us tonight." Jesus said, "I am with you always." Isn't this just a habit we have fallen into? And what does it really mean? To me, it is as superfluous as praying, "Oh, Lord, keep me breathing while I am alive on this earth!"

If we were really *thinking*, if we had really alerted ourselves to Him as He is, we would begin our prayers by thanking Him that He *is* always with us! To some of you, particularly some adults who might be reading this book, this may sound glib. If it does, I'll just have to be willing to be misunderstood by you; because with all my heart I believe we must begin to learn how to be actively *with* God — certainly when we pray. To the individual heart He whispers, "I will never leave you nor forsake you." To the group He spoke just as specifically: "Where two or three are gathered together in My Name, there I will be in their midst."

Do you think I'm splitting hairs? Doesn't God understand about our habits? Doesn't He listen to the very beat of our hearts? Yes. But remember, I have already said that it is for *our* sakes that we need to learn how to be with Him. It is for us that our mental and spiritual alertness becomes necessary. There is always a calming influence when people stop to pray, no matter what they say or whether or not it is read or extemporized. But how much more value there would be if we realized that we do *not* "go into God's presence" when we stop to address Him — we are already in it! How many times have you heard people pray, "Oh, Lord, we come into your Presence, etc."? How is this possible? What we really do is to quiet our hearts so that we *remember* that we are already with Him.

One university senior surprised everyone in the group with which he was praying by saying, "Lord Jesus, we've all been praying here for ten minutes or so, and I'm still so noisy inside from the kind of day I've had, that I'm not realizing You're here with us. Will You please calm me down?"

This, to me, was authentic. It changed the whole atmosphere of that group. Up to that point the students had just been "spieling" words. No one was insincere, consciously or unconsciously. It was just dead. What a tragedy, when the Lord of Life was right there waiting to be recognized!

Rosalind Rinker's definition of prayer is this: "Prayer is a dialogue between two persons who love each other."

Could anything be more to the point? If you're in conversation with the one you love, do you just ramble on with yards of phrases you've heard other people say — filling the silence with a stream of almost nothing? Girls who talk this much, without thinking through what they say, seldom get asked for the second date. Fellows who ramble on without a breather for the girl to get in a word edgewise, have to keep on hunting up new telephone numbers. God isn't like that. He has been putting up with our inattention since time began. He keeps coming back again and again, always trying to make us aware of Him, but what a glorious thing our relationship with Him could be if we really gave Him our undivided attention! If we spent our conversations with Him in a caring, thoughtful frame of mind and heart.

Conversation, of course, implies that two people are involved. How much time do you allow God to speak *in reply* to what you have just said to Him? We storm Him for guidance and never wait one second in the silence to hear what He might have to say in answer to our request.

As with every other subject in this book, if you know God, your prayer times can begin to come alive in direct proportion to how much you are *thinking*. Try talking to Him as *you* talk. Don't be afraid not to be saying something every minute. Find out for yourself by entering into a real conversation with God, how *to be with Him* in prayer.

Our moments of conscious prayer are not the only times we need to know how to be with God. Paul wrote that we were to pray without ceasing. What did he mean by this? Surely he did not mean that we were to neglect our work, our study, our driving, in order to do nothing whatever but form the sentences which we call prayer. His provocative line makes the bridge, as I see it, between what we have already said concerning actual prayer and just learning to be with God in the daily round.

"Pray without ceasing."

Could it be that our entire lives hold the potential of *being* prayer? Could it be that prayer is also a state of being? I believe so. I am seeing more every day that my life can be in a perpetual state of God-consciousness, even during the times when I am busily concentrating on the grocery list, a chapter in a book, or driving in heavy traffic. Is this because I am a superior spiritual being? What a ridiculous thought! Neither are you. We are all equal here. Anyone holds within himself the capacity for knowing God. We all have been given His Spirit, if we have received Him as our Saviour. The Bible tells us that His Spirit within us will witness to the same Spirit within another person. His Spirit never contradicts Himself and always recognizes Christ. In fact, as I understand God's Word on the subject, the Spirit of Christ is actually living and willing to function in each of His followers. His Spirit even *cultivates* our faith as we are open to Him. As we are alert to Him. As we are aware of His presence. Doesn't it stand to reason, then, that *except* as we fail to live under the control of His Spirit, we can all come to realize constant communion with God?

Once more, I do not mean by this that we must always go about consciously thinking about Him. Real faith is not that we keep our minds on God every minute, but that we have finally caught on to the fact that God never allows His mind to wander for one second from us! Real thought on this truth breeds confidence in Him, makes daily and natural to us the fact of His constant Presence with us, steadily increases our feeling of being at home with Him.

"Pray without ceasing."

Paul was a busy man, busier than most of us; and this potent sentence flowed from his own experience. He had come to know *how to be with God* under all conditions. As I wrote through my book, *Beloved World*, retelling the story of God and people in today's language, I found myself experiencing for the first time real kinship with the people whose stories I attempted to communicate. It requires no stretch of my imagination now to think of Peter and John and James, and even Samson and Isaiah, as *being* my brothers; as actually *being* people who now are perhaps in converse, not only with God, but with Jesus, His mother Mary, Browning, Chesterton, Peter Marshall, my own father. Writing *Beloved World* forced me to find out for myself what these people might really have been like. They are all real to me now; but perhaps Paul, more than anyone else, "became a human being" for me. I had always admired him, sometimes disliked him for being so strict, but now Paul, in a particular way, is my brother.

Here was a man who had perhaps the most difficulty of anyone in the New Testament story, making the big leap from his old, swaggering, self-confident, even arrogant life, into the humility and balance and dependence of his new life in Christ. I became so absorbed in the utter humanity of Paul that I now do not think it is far-fetched to believe that Jesus *had* to do something as drastic as He did on the road to Damascus in order to get the attention of this highly educated, near-tyrannical Saul. Everything Saul of Tarsus did, he did to an extreme. It so happened that his background was what we would call "good." He was, by his own admission, "a Hebrew of the Hebrews." This would be similar to having a zealous young man now proclaim himself to be a "conservative of the conservatives." Not just doctrinally, of course, but also psychologically and for all practical reasons. By his own circle of relatives and academic associates, Saul was rated "tops." His superiors felt he had tremendous possibilities, real potential. They took full advantage of his boundless energy and ambition and his devotion to his religion. At the very moment Jesus appeared to him on the road to Damascus, he was on his way briskly, even fanatically, to do away with those Christians whom he sincerely believed to be heretics. The men in power were making full use of Saul's talents, ambitions and fanaticism.

But Jesus Christ, risen from the dead, appeared to this young man on his murderous mission to Damascus, and appeared so brightly and so definitely that Saul was literally knocked down in the dusty road! More important, however, his tremendous, compulsive ego was knocked down, and he was literally blinded to all that he had believed he saw up to that point. I now believe that much more than Saul's physical sight was gone (and this physical blindness didn't last long). The important thing is that, once and for all, Saul of Tarsus was never able to see himself in the same relation to God and his fellow human beings again. Out of his sudden blindness came a genuine, permanent new birth, and with it, permanent new *sight*. Up to that moment he had felt the steady, sometimes exhausting, but always stimulating drive to "help" the Lord God of Israel out of His difficulties. Saul of Tarsus was going to be one of the Lord's great doers.

Then Jesus came to him, and all of this changed. From that moment the brilliant young man walked another way, in a totally new attitude of heart. He no longer considered himself essential to God, but without a doubt God would always be essential to Paul. Even his name was changed. Saul of Tarsus was a talented, dynamic driver — egotistical about his much *doing*. The Lord's new man, Paul, spent the remainder of his earthly life learning how to *be*. And to Paul, all being was *being with Christ*. More than any other Apostle, Paul's life bore fruit for the Kingdom of God, but perhaps also more than any other Apostle, Paul learned that God and *being* were one and the same. He founded churches in the pagan lands where the other disciples refused to go or didn't think of going. He taught the immature Christians in these new brotherhoods how to "grow up" in Christ, writing them letters of admonition and instruction and encouragement, which we still use today. The Lord could trust Paul with the difficult situations. His lifetime of service has never been challenged. It still stands as the supreme example of a life spent in loving friendship and work for God.

What did Paul think about it all? What was his own estimate of his long life of hardship and persecution and travail? What did he have to say about his success? Did he boast about his loyalty? Did he keep track of the numbers he had reached for Jesus Christ? What *did* Paul say about his life? His comment on it, right from the center of activity, right while he was living it, was simply this: "For me *to live is* Christ."

How different is this statement, in truth, from "Pray without ceasing"? Aren't they basically the same thing? Wasn't Paul able to instruct us to pray without ceasing only because he had learned that true *being* and God are inseparable?

Once you and I get it clear that "in Him we (do) live and breathe and have our being," we will no longer have to work on being with God.

It will become not only the natural thing to do, it will be the inevitable.

9 *Finding Out God's Idea for Your Life*

When you think of God's idea (or will) for your life, do everything you can to convince yourself that Jesus, because He *was* God as Man, spoke the truth when He said: "I have come that you might have life, and have it more abundantly."

God's idea for everyone is *abundant* life; and *abundant* means "possessing in great quantity, having great plenty."

This, of course, does not mean that we are all going to be as rich as the Kennedys or the Rockefellers. It does mean, though, that we can discover the kind of life which will completely satisfy our longings. Over and over again I hear Christians worry aloud for fear a close, personal relationship with God is going to spoil something. This, if we believe what Jesus said, is simply *impossible*. Either an intimate, hour-by-hour walk with God is the way to *finding* life at its fullest, or the Son of God was wrong. There simply is no middle ground. No third possibility.

It is God's idea, then, that you possess life in "great quantity, having great plenty." Do you believe that? Or are you one of the thousands of young people who shy away from commitment to Jesus Christ for fear He will send you to a jungle to exist on a missionary's pittance?

Now be reasonable. God is. In the first place, isn't it a careless generalization to think that God is interested *only* in what we call "full-time Christian service"? Just because missionaries spend their time in the actual propagation of the Gospel, does this mean that God is interested exclusively in their work? I think not. God is just as interested in the man on the assembly line who inserts the gears in the jeep a missionary may use, as He is in the missionary. In fact, even if a missionary doesn't use that jeep, God's interest in that mechanic does not diminish one iota. The Bible tells us that "God so loved the *world*." He does not love men and women in Christian work any more than He loves professional basketball players or housewives.

Perhaps it would be well, right here, for us to get one thing straight: God's idea is that *everyone* should be in full-

58

time Christian service! Where is there a more important opportunity than in being a mother to growing children? A father of growing children actually forms the child's God-image until the child is old enough to have his own. Could anything be more important to God than that a parent live up to these high callings?

Please don't misunderstand me. In no way do I mean to diminish the sacrifice and wonderfully creative work of missionaries, either at home or in foreign service. Realizing, of course, that they are people just like us, I am almost in awe of some of them. Still I feel sure that any balanced, authentic missionary anywhere on the globe would join me fully in attempting to persuade you that God's call to you is not always going to be to the specialized field of service where your salary happens to be paid by a mission board.

God's call is to *Himself* first.

And fully aware that I may bring down some criticism on my graying head from a few well-meaning souls whose specific vocation keeps them trying to persuade young people to enter professional Christian service, I still must make myself clear on this point: I have become convinced from having been present at many missionary services that we *dare* not make use of emotional manipulation here! It is just as important that you be sure that God is *not* calling you to the foreign field or the ministry as it is for you to be sure that He is.

I know of nothing more exciting than to talk with a young person who is quietly certain that God has called him or her into some particular branch of Christian service. This experience is as gratifying as it is heart-breaking to observe the false guilt and confusion in the minds and hearts of those who have "responded" from whipped-up human pressure.

A woman in her fifties wrote this to me not long ago: "For almost thirty years I have kept quiet about the torment in my heart over a 'call' I think I disobeyed when I was young. I remember the night as though it were last night. I was attending a summer youth conference, and on the last night of the week we had a powerful missionary speaker. He painted the horrors of heathenism so that I felt as though I was going to choke. He told us about the suffering and the sickness among the natives on his field. He berated us for all the plenty we have here, and told us we were selfish and disloyal to God if we kept on living in such luxury and failed to answer God's call. By the time he asked for those among us who would give our lives for the sake of Christ among these natives, I would have had to be tied to my seat to keep from almost running up that aisle! I began at once to train for the foreign mission field. But before I graduated from school, illness struck our family and I had to go home. Later, I too became ill. Then I met my husband and, although we have had all these years of service to the Lord together in our church and among the unfortunate people in the slums of our city, I still feel such guilt over that 'call' I failed to follow that I sometimes fear I will lose my mind. We have raised four fine children, and two of our sons have churches of their own now. I try to tell myself that no modern mission board would have accepted me anyway, due to my poor health in my twenties. But the thought keeps haunting me that maybe a board would have accepted me *then* when they were not so strict as now."

My heart goes out to this woman in a rush of sympathy! Her guilt is *false*, obviously. God guides us by closed doors as well as open ones. He, and He alone, knows whether He is doing the calling at a missionary meeting. He, and He alone, knows whether it is merely the tender heart of a young person, responding with love toward those less fortunate, which prompts the "response." If it is this, He seems always to begin closing doors. Sometimes, however, young people push through. Anyone connected with missionary personnel will tell you quickly that the missionaries who crack up on the field are almost always those who should not have gone in the first place. God is never desperate for mere numbers! He can always do much more through one or two persons whom He has called specifically, than through a dozen who respond from stirred-up emotions or as a career only.

There is no point expounding on the need for young men whom God has called to enter the ministry, *or* the futility of their entering it "for Mother's sake," or because it holds the promise of a refined profession. Both issues are obvious.

60

God does need real shepherds in the pulpits of His churches, and missionaries on the field, but I find nothing in His character which ever tries to confuse us on any point. He says plainly that He will tell us whether we are "to turn to the right or to the left." Until we are sure, we should not jump in either direction.

I can now hear you say, "But what about me? I've got to know *now* which school to attend. I don't have enough money to wait." I can only say in reply that God knows about your financial situation, too. The point we are attempting to make here is this: *God is always calling everyone to Himself.* This stirs our hearts and our emotions. It is quite possible that along with His call to you to come to *Him* for love's sake, He is also urging you toward some specific Christian field of service. This is quite possible, but I cannot feel fully honest with you if I do not also remind you that He needs committed Christian doctors, dentists, plumbers, bank tellers, artists, musicians, lawyers, school teachers, department store clerks, farmers and carpenters, too.

The purpose of this book, don't forget, is mainly to start you *thinking*. I really have to control myself when some well-meaning person says to me, "Oh, I wish I could serve God the way you do!" I don't serve God any more importantly than the housewife whose name is known only to the members of her church and the neighbors on her block, who guides her children with patience and balance, and loves and cares for the needs of her husband as Christ instructed.

We miss the point entirely if we confuse quality with quantity here. More people happen to know that I write books about God simply because it is customary to put the author's name on the books he writes. But this in no way measures the *quality* of my service. If you are unknown, this likewise is no criterion of your service. A successful minister gets most of the publicity and glory, but I have a theory that if God has a special pinnacle in heaven for anyone, it will be for really good ministers' *wives*. The successful business executive gets his name in *Time* magazine, but he might be in a dreadful predicament if it weren't for his personal secretary whose name never breaks into print. Thousands of people know the name of the much-in-demand head of a certain Christian institution, but to those who actually work in this organization the real man of God is the humble, unpublicized engineer who tends the furnace and keeps the electrical system working!

God needs young people with balanced, educated minds and consecrated hearts on the mission fields and in the pulpits and behind the professors' desks in Christian colleges. God needs young people with balanced, educated minds and consecrated hearts in offices and public schoolrooms, in hospitals and factories. God needs young people with balanced, educated minds and consecrated hearts — period.

God's idea for your life will be made clear to you in plenty of time. This I can guarantee, because of what I know about God. Of course, we need to seek His guidance. But even here we can go overboard. If you have studied the Scriptures, *recognizing* God's voice will be a great deal simpler. He will never guide you toward any goal that goes against what He has said to you in the Bible. This is one sure way: Test your guidance by the Scriptures first of all. Then act as though you really believe He came to live His life *in* you when you received Him as your Saviour. You now have access to an intelligence *enlightened* from within by the Holy Spirit of God Himself. When you talk to God about the matter of discovering His idea for your life, take time to *listen* to what He may be saying to you. While we can never rely alone on what we might believe to be the inner voice, without checking it out with the Scriptures, He *does* speak. But His voice is a "still small voice," and so we have to calm down and listen. Finally, He knows just how confusing the issues really are for you. He knows when you are complicating them by out-of-control emotions, stubbornness, or even ignorance or innocence. He knows you haven't lived through many years yet, and so, if the situation is unusually puzzling, I firmly believe we can ask and expect Him to show us through concrete, providential *circumstances*.

If your heart is open to God's idea for your life, and if you are still in doubt on a major point, ask Him to give you such unmistakable evidence one way or the other that it's almost impossible to miss His point.

But we all do miss it now and then! Even the most sincere among us, even the most alert. When and if you make an honest mistake, God knows that, too. Don't waste your good energies by heaping foolish, false guilt on yourself. This is one place where we *must* give ourselves a chance to find out all we can possibly learn about the true nature of God. If you really know Him as He is, you know Him as a true Redeemer — not just where the sin question is concerned, but where your circumstances are concerned as well. Our God is the kind of Redeemer God who will make good, creative *use* even of our mistakes. With Him nothing ever needs to be wasted. But it will appear to be a waste unless we know Him well enough to count, from the moment we see our error, on His ability to redeem even our bad judgments.

God's idea for your life is a peaceful idea. He is not the author of confusion. Where there is a flagrant mess and a seemingly hopeless mix-up, *this has not been God's idea.* "My peace I leave with you," Jesus said. "I know the thoughts that I think toward you, saith the Lord; they are thoughts of peace and not of evil, to give you an *expected end.*"

God's ultimate idea for you is peaceful, controlled, sane. The confusion and the trouble spring from sources other than God. He warned us that there would be trouble, but He also left His peace with us. Paul goes one step farther: "He is our peace."

I have no sympathy whatever with adults who minimize the torment possible in the hearts and minds of young people trying to decide the major issues of their lives. Just as some thoughtless (and forgetful) adults try to minimize your heartaches by labeling your romance "puppy love," so some of them will try to brush you off in the area of your dilemmas and decisions. Here you have to show a maturity deeper than theirs, regardless of the difference in your years. You will simply have to forgive them and accept them as being thoughtless, and as having forgotten, apparently, what it was like at your age. God did not need to come down here to earth and become a Baby, and then a growing Boy, and then a Teenager, and then a young Man so that *He* would know how it feels to be you. But He *did* it, and I am convinced that one reason He did it was so that *you* would know that He knows how it feels to be you.

He does. "I know the thoughts I think toward you . . .

thoughts of peace and not of evil." *Evil*, remember, is *live* spelled backwards! God wants you to *live*.

Waiting is difficult, especially for the young. But God will never, never try to mix you up. If you do all you can do to discover Him as He really is; if you have begun to assume your responsibilities as a growing young adult, in school preparation as well as learning to make choices; if you have thought through your side of things, you can be certain God has His ideas all straight for you. In fact, His idea for your life is all set, even if you have been a slacker. But no one, even the most thoughtful among us, can expect Him to give us His ideas for our lives in lightning flashes emblazoned across the night sky of our self-made confusions. He is much more interested in reforming your character, in teaching you how to *live* abundantly, than He is in the exact corner of the exact street or the exact spot on the exact foreign field where you are to spend your days.

Always, always, our God will be more interested in what we *are*, than what we do.

10 Finding Out About Real Popularity

The dictionary definition of popularity implies a thing or a person "commonly liked, approved, found praiseworthy."

Surely there is nothing wrong with your being "commonly liked, approved, or found praiseworthy." This is all good, *providing* it does not distort you in the process. Also, there is nothing essentially wrong with someone other than you being "commonly liked, approved, or found praiseworthy," *unless* his popularity also distorts you with jealousy, envy, and rebellion.

I even remember the shape of the head and the set of the shoulders of the fellow who was considered the most popular boy in high school when I was there. I, along with everyone else in the school, was duly impressed with this young man's *popularity*. He stood a magnificent head above all the other boys in all ways — except scholastically, and that didn't seem to bother him or the teachers much. He even had initials for a name, instead of an ordinary name like the rest of us. J.A., his initials were, and no doubt they appeared on more girls' textbooks than any other set of initials in academic history. At least in the history of our school. J.A. didn't walk; he swaggered beautifully. The lesser ones among us felt no ill will toward him because he never had time to speak to us; we really believed he *was* just that busy. After all, it took a lot of time to be J.A. because *popularity* just naturally takes time, we figured.

Oh, me . . . J.A.! I remember him well . . . the most popular boy in the whole school. But you know something? Since graduation, I've never heard anything about how old J.A. turned out! If he turned out to be famous, he changed his name from J.A. If he "didn't turn out well," as my Grandmother would have said, I haven't heard a word about that either.

But I've had J.A. on my mind a lot these last few days as I've been thinking through what I would say to you in this chapter on *Finding Out About Real Popularity*, so let's consider him a moment longer right now. This boy was so handsome, so athletic, such a personality-kid with the girls, so looked-up-to by almost everyone in our large high school, I can't help wondering who was there to catch him when and if life outside knocked him down the first time. This is not funny. Everything came so easily to him during those four years in which he was king of his little world, life as it really is could well have dealt him a wicked blow — and soon.

If I have implied that J.A. was a bad sort, I have misled you. He was not. In retrospect, I don't seem to remember that I felt he was particularly egotistical — or "conceited" as we said then. He just seemed *so busy* being popular. I don't remember seeing the boy smile much; in fact, he was probably ahead of his time by about 25 years, because some of the dead-pan quasi "beats" now make me think of J.A. Oh, he had his hair cut in the latest style then — long and slicked back with Sta-Comb. (I'm now 46, in case you've forgotten!) But his face was not only handsome, it was like the faces of some contemporary young men, almost expressionless as I recall it now. But I don't think he was assuming this brand of serious countenance, I think he was serious — serious about being *popular*. We all thought he was terrific (whatever we meant by that) and we had him thinking it too. He took his burden of popularity as a solemn responsibility. Now and then he honestly felt he owed a small, benign smile to one of the younger among us — the unglamorous, the non-popular. He didn't make us feel *unpopular;* we just knew that unless we were accepted into J.A.'s inner circle we were among the non-popular. He was, I'm sure, a thoroughly conscientious, good sort. But for that boy to enter a large university, or step into a competitive business office where no one had heard that he was "the most popular boy," the "king" of our high school, could have been a shocking experience. I hope he weathered the switch, because I'm sure there was one — many, perhaps.

I have brought up the matter of J.A. hoping it would stimulate you to do some thinking — about yourself if you happen to be "the most popular one," or about the one who is that in your immediate world. If you have been resenting someone because you have never achieved his or her popularity, slow down a minute and think it through. Perhaps that person needs your prayers. If he or she is "too busy being popular" to realize the need of your friendship, prayer is always in order — in love and understanding. Life "outside" is going to be very, very different for that person; unless, of course, he does what so many people do who thrive on their own popularity — work at becoming a big shot in his lodge or his church group, just so he'll feel familiar somewhere, even though the competition is rough at the office.

Now, at this point, do you have the idea that I'm deprecating, making fun of popularity? If so, either you haven't been reading carefully, or I'm not writing carefully.

Popularity is not a bad thing. It can be totally creative, in fact, depending upon the degree of *objectivity* or *subjectivity* of the person or persons involved. If you are not popular, and resent those who are, you are, of course, being *subjective*. You are not accepting yourself as you are, nor them as they are. Subjective attitudes cloy and clutch; objectivity accepts and frees. In no way am I suggesting that you should not try to be popular, *if* by doing so you still remain your true self. Of course, if you don't happen to be the type that magnetizes, you will only make yourself ridiculous by trying. If you are not the strong, dominant male, accept yourself as you are and trust God to find friends for you who will like you because you are you. By trusting God, I don't mean you are to sit on the sidelines and wait for someone to fall at your feet, declaring you are just the shy, weighty type sought for. Go out to people in any way that is natural to *you*. It may not be natural for you to have a cheery smile for everyone you meet on the campus or the street. If it isn't, then when you do smile, make it real.

If you are the *popular type* — much liked, deeply approved, widely accepted — even looked up to, God will give you (if He hasn't already) the kind of true objectivity that will make your popularity creative. There is a wide difference between being "well known" and truly popular. The "well known" young person is not always well-liked. And I believe this difference should be thought through carefully. The young woman who is much in demand as a "date" may not be a respected person. She can be — we must not make this a hard and fast rule, lest we tumble into judging and self-righteousness. But you will discover more and more as you grow older that what appears one way may be entirely another upon closer inspection. "All that glitters is not gold," to drag up an old cliché from J.A.'s day and mine.

If you are well-liked, popular, *respected*, thank God and be willing to shoulder the full responsibility of so much attention. The popular student or working young person has an added responsibility that is not always easy to carry. If you are popular, you are somewhat, at least, in the public eye. Your life, your disposition, your grades, your work must pass muster. When people honor you with their love and affection and respect, honor them with your best intentions fulfilled.

We have used the word *respect* twice now, and I believe it is the key to *true popularity*. A person may be extremely well known, even famous, without being truly *popular*. I spent a long time one evening talking with a lonely, confused football star who complained that even though everyone thought he was "great stuff" on the field, even though the grandstands rocked when he was sent into the game, on campus nobody seemed to like him. (Perhaps much of his problem lay in his own self-love, but it also lay in the fact that his fellow students hadn't bothered to try to identify with him. No one had offered him a real friendship. The girls felt flattered when he asked them for a date, but no one wore his pin.) His disposition was prickly; he was not a good student and, although he was well known, he was not truly *respected*.

True popularity, whether it is among five thousand people or two or three, must include *respect*. People are just not going to *like* you merely because you are beautiful, or handsome, or brilliant, or well read, or a sensational quarterback.

True popularity must be *earned*. It may not be necessary to work at it as hard as J.A. did, but it must be earned. By this I mean that the kind of popularity that comes with a flare, or on the jet-stream of a fad, will be passing. At best, popularity must be considered passing. A baseball star begins to see his popularity sail out over the left field wall when he reaches thirty-five. He may still be a good clutch-hitter, he may be worth much to the younger players as a friend and counselor, but when he slows down on the field, the fans soon begin to look elsewhere for a reason to yell.

Singers, actors, popular musicians, popular music itself — all have a moment in the sun and then pass away, sometimes into oblivion.

Over-exposure is an item here. When I was your age a popular song lasted for years and years, despite the fact that radio was climbing to its peak. Now, if a song becomes popular, it is worn through to the other side of the record by a nation-load of DJ's who *over-expose* it into almost overnight nothingness. There is a point for you here, if you find yourself currently well-liked and popular. Don't push it. Just be natural. Just be yourself, your best self.

Obviously, we can't all be cover-girls and cover-boys. You and I can't help it if we weren't born conforming to today's western standards of physical beauty or charm. But there is a Magnet abroad in the world, and His Name is Jesus Christ. Anyone in whom this Christ lives His life day by day is bound to be more attractive than those in whom He does not have the freedom to live. This, of course, doesn't mean all Christians are heading for inevitable popularity. Some Christians are appalling! A young, attractive socialite met Christ through one of God's wise old saints several years ago in New York City. "But, Mr. Mosely," she exclaimed, after attending church with him, "most of those Christians are so dull and unattractive looking!" The old saint grinned at her and replied: "I agree, my dear, but just think what they'd be like *without* Jesus!"

So, whatever we are — He improves upon it. In the area of your disposition alone the presence of Christ in your life *can*, if you are cooperating with Him, make all the difference in the world in your popularity. The most popular girl on my floor in one college dorm was not particularly attractive. On top of that, she didn't do any of the things the rest of us thought we had to do in order to "live it up" at college. *But* this gal had a most attractive disposition and sense of humor. I didn't see her again for twenty years, until one afternoon, in a bookstore in the East, she turned up at one of my autographing parties. I found out then why she had been the most well-liked gal on the dorm floor where I lived — she was a *practicing* Christian. She didn't mow us down with her faith; she lived it, and we all loved her and respected her. There were some other Christians in the dorm too, but they were "creeps." They held themselves aloof from us, let it be known that *they* didn't do this and *they* didn't do that. This girl didn't either, but she loved us anyway, just the way her Lord did.

Remember, remember, remember that Jesus Christ did say, "I, if *I* be lifted up . . . will *draw* . . ." When we are *attractive*, we *draw*. With Him in charge of our dispositions (an area where many Christians keep him out *religiously*), we will be well liked.

There is no area in your life where you must be more realistic than the area of your personal appeal to other people. True popularity is a much-to-be-desired state. But just desiring it isn't enough. We must want it enough to earn the respect and love of other people, and then we must want enough to keep it to assume the responsibility that it inevitably brings.

True popularity cannot be learned from charm magazines or self-development courses. It comes (in varying degrees, of course) according to whether or not you are being your best self. Some best selves are naturally more attractive than others. But regardless of the degree of natural charm which you may have, Christ's life within you can shine you up.

With Him anyone can be his best self.

11 Finding Out About Your Parents

"I don't ever expect to know my parents — not really. I just steel myself to go along until I'm out from under their control. I don't think anyone on this campus hates the thought of Christmas holidays at home as much as I hate it. Oh, it's not that they're *mean* to me, but they're just so strict that I have to make too much of an adjustment from campus to home."

The college sophomore who was airing her feelings about what she called her "old-fashioned" parents, brushed back the heavy lock of hair that had slipped its moorings in the "teased" stack on her pretty head, and sighed.

"Anyone here on campus can tell you I'm not a rebel. I don't break rules here. I just hate being treated like I'm still ten years old, and that's the way my folks treat me! Here we are treated like adults — as though we have enough sense to assume *some* responsibility at least."

This was an old, old story to me, but still as important as ever. The line that stuck with me was this one: "I don't ever expect to know my parents — not really."

Without realizing it, this gal had sounded a deep note. Parents *are* knowable, no matter what you may think. Parents are knowable, because parents are people. It shouldn't be true, but unfortunately it is, that parents are often extremely difficult to know. But then, so are their offspring. Why is this? The answer is obvious, if we really think it through. Big, high, thick walls of complicated emotions block the knowing. Misunderstandings dating back to childhood, on both sides, when everyone expected too much of everyone else. Carelessness on both sides. Lack of *identification* on both sides.

This last point — identification — *can* be, if either parent or child begins to practice it, the happy bulldozer which will knock down those walls, or most of them. It is as unrealistic to say that many parents are *not* over-strict, as it is to say that no young person ever takes advantage of his parents. Young people do take advantage of their parents, and parents can

71

be and often are over-strict. These are simply the facts. But something can be done.

Too often, nothing is. My mail continues to be loaded with letters from women (occasionally men), in middle life and beyond, whose life patterns are still twisted because no real bond of *communication* was ever established between them and their parents. The wall stayed up for one reason or another. The happy bulldozer of *identification* was never put into operation.

Before we go into the tremendous possibilities of your beginning to identify with your parents, perhaps it would be well if we faced one more major fact: Just because you are your mother's daughter or your father's son does not mean that life at home should be or should have been a beautiful, no-conflict, halcyon thing. Where people of differing personalities and ages live together under the same roof, trouble spots are inevitable. And where does one find a wider age span than in the average family at home? I don't wonder that there are troublesome times between parents and their children; I wonder that there aren't more of them. After all, two generations naturally have difficulty seeing things alike. Even when there is *communication*, just the age difference brings an almost automatic difference in viewpoints and interests.

But if even one person begins to use the golden key of identification, the communication lines grow stronger, and much of the misunderstanding can drop away. When we *identify* with someone else, we put ourselves in that person's spot for a moment, attempting to see as he sees, hear as he hears, react as he might react according to where *he* is, not according to where we are, nor how he has made us feel.

For example, if someone has hurt you, spoken harshly to you or about you, you *can*, if you are not too self-preoccupied, try to understand what it was in your personality or behavior that made the other person react against you in that way. This is not easy. The human thing to do under such circumstances is to strike back, or at least to sink into a temporarily comfortable nest of self-pity. Self-pity or retribution can only bring temporary relief, however. In the long run, anyone knows they bring more chaos.

Your parents *are people* — faulty, lovable, sometimes

thoughtless human beings. If your Dad has "dressed you down" for that ticket you got for speeding during your vacation at home, it could be that he over-did it. Maybe he lost his temper, and this, of course, is not only hard on him, but also hard on you. You know you are guilty; you did speed, and you did get the ticket. What should you do when your father blows his stack at you? Should you deny the charges and blame the cop? Should you hang your head and sulk, and begin to count the days until you can get out from under his roof again? Should you remind him that he also got a ticket for speeding last winter and that it was worse than yours because the roads were slick when his foot got too heavy on the accelerator?

How about *identifying* with him? How about trying to analyze the situation, after, of course, you have said you are sorry and that you realize what a dangerous and foolhardy thing you did. (Remember, this is not just to pacify your father. It is needed to reinforce your inner man too!) Seriously, are you interested enough in real maturity — for that matter, are you interested enough in your own father as a human being — to make an effort to *understand* why he became so upset? We are not sitting in judgment on Pop. Chances are, he did ride you overly hard. But there can be only more confusion if you ride him back. What can you do?

I used this hypothetical illustration at a fraternity house at a Kansas University several years ago, and a sophomore interrupted me to share an almost identical real happening at his family home the year before: "I hadn't thought of it as something I could have done earlier, when the whole ruckus started," the young man said, "but this whole business of *identification* just up and hit me, as it were! I thought I'd have to interrupt you sooner to tell you what happened to me, it's so much like your illustration. You see, I got a ticket for speeding during Thanksgiving vacation at home. My Dad flew in all directions. The only thinking I did was to wonder why he flew quite so hard, since, as a rule, he is a mild-mannered gent. Other than that, I just flew back at him. That night, up in my old room at home, where I went to mope and nurse my injured feelings, I decided I'd look through my old dresser drawers just to see how much of my junk Mom had left in them. Most of it was there, but what caught my eye

73

was a pile of old scrapbooks and albums she had put there, too, after I had left for college. I started leafing through them, and about halfway through my Dad's business scrapbook an old yellowed clipping fell out on the floor. It hadn't been pasted in, just stuck there. I read it. And then I felt so sorry, I wanted to cry. It was about my Dad when he was two years older than I am now. He had struck and killed a little five-year-old boy with his car. Oh, it wasn't Dad's fault; he was cleared of the charges, but I guess he never forgot it. His 'top blowing' was more than temper or annoyance with me. I saw his old panic in it as I stared at that clipping. He wanted to impress the danger of speeding on me so I wouldn't have to go through the tortures he must still sometimes go through over that kid he killed."

The young man choked up, and finished quickly. "I guess — well, I guess, like you just said, I began to *identify* with Dad."

Family misunderstandings will not always be handled as forcefully and as dramatically as this, but the point I want to make is that the reading of these pages *can* bring you to the same place this old clipping brought that boy. His genuine concern for his Dad began a whole new relationship between them. From that night on he made an effort in other things to see both his parents' points of view.

Now, identification is not an original idea with me, nor any other mere human being. *It is God's idea.*

When He confined Himself to human life — invaded human history as the Baby Jesus — He performed the act of perfect *identification*. No one can ever say that God does not know what it's like to be a trouble-ridden, lonely, rejected human being. He does. He knew it all along, but He took the time and trouble to get into this thing with us so that *we* would know that He knows.

There is a lot to be said to parents along this line of identification, because too often they forget (conveniently or unconsciously) what it's like to be young. I am writing these pages to young people themselves, however, so any interested parents will have to make the application for themselves. I will settle with saying this to them: You could save yourself and your children many miserable hours of heartache and confusion if you stopped more often to remember that what you call rebellion in them, *might* be what you called fear or insecurity in yourself when you were their age. What you now admonish as stubbornness *might* be the same inner panic that bruised some of your early years. What you label as irresponsible in your young person could be due to the fact that *you*, like your parent before you, have not taught that young person to make choices.

I will stop now with parents, and turn to you as young people. Even if your parents have not caught on to the wonder of identification, you *can*. Many young people have irresponsible, immature parents. Just because a child is born to a man and woman is no indication that these parents have suddenly reached full maturity. So, perhaps right now would be the best possible time for you, as their offspring, to have a good, long, careful, objective look at your parents. What are they really like?

What, in their past lives, caused them to be this way? Were they poor and now have money? If so, this could mean they may lay unreasonable demands on you, insisting that you live up to what they might have done with their lives, had they received your opportunities. If they are talented, they can be determined that you will be equally so, or more. If your mother's human father was a tyrant, then it stands to reason that if no one has corrected her misconception, the God she follows may be a "tyrant God," too. She may have turned you against Him quite innocently. If so, this does not excuse her, but it does *explain* her somewhat. If you are a preacher's kid, you quite possibly have been forced into an unnatural way of life. You may not have been allowed to think for yourself, for fear you might come up with something the good church members wouldn't like. This is not right, but it is often the way it is. Would it help if you tried to imagine your mother and father stretching themselves over that big chasm between you and the good brothers and sisters for all those years? Chances are, they felt they could control you more easily than they could control the board members or the ladies' auxiliary, so *you* got the twists in your personality.

There is no point in holding grudges against parents for any of the above reasons at this late date. Grudges harm the

75

holder much more than they harm anyone else. Try letting them go for a minute, as you look with some of God's understanding and love at those people who are your parents. If He lives in you, remember, you have access to His *knowing* and His *understanding*.

It has not been the highest thing for your parents to have been overly strict with you, but what about your father as a young man? How much of the world did he see before he settled down with Mom? How much did she see, for that matter, before she settled down with Pop? Could it be that they wish their parents had kept a closer check on them, and they are now determined you won't go through the same experiences? They may well be overdoing it, but be *objective* about them. You may not see much change in *them* for all your objectivity, but I can guarantee you will see change in *yourself*. You will at least be rid of a lot of your self-pity, resentment and rebellion.

It would be an untruth to say that it is *easy* to accept parents as they are. It is not easy. It is the hardest kind of acceptance there is. We all want our parents to be tops. In fact, we want them to be perfect, at least when we're young. Since no one is, this is just one more quirk we have to outgrow. It was a shocker the day I realized that my Mother and Dad were merely human. When I relaxed about it, the relief began. Result? I ended up loving them both still more, because I realized that all the Prices were possessors of faulty human nature together!

I have frequently told young people that if they don't begin to grow up in Christ *now*, in their late teens and early twenties, they will end up being as much trouble to their children as their parents have been to them. Everyone caught on to this and laughed. But it is true. Some of you may be parents already; most of you will be in a matter of a few years. Won't you want understanding from your offspring? Of course you will. But will you deserve it if you haven't learned how to identify with your parents first? For that matter, will your children ever hear of such a thing, unless they happen to find a book like this on your shelf some day, or better yet, learn it straight from you?

A few years difference in age is, in itself, a mighty barrier. Just being a parent can be a barrier! A young lady aged sixteen once said to me: "Oh, I can tell you anything, Genie, you're not old like my mother!" When I asked her mother's age, the dear woman turned out to be three years younger than I! What made it easier for the gal to confide in me? There may have been other reasons, but certainly I *seemed* younger to her merely because she and I were not mothers!

Think about your parents. Think, think, think. They are people, too, just like you and me. They are people with sometimes frightened inner selves, with insecurities, with doubts, anxieties, *and* hearts. If your parents lay what you objectively see to be unreasonable demands on you, it can be due, of course, to their out-sized egos. They want *their* offspring to excel. This is not fair to you, because what they should want is for you to be the best *you* possible, even if you don't excel. This will give you a chance to be natural and relaxed, and will free those possibly latent talents in you which have been choked back by fear of not living up to what Mom and Dad expect. Can you change this wrong attitude of theirs? Most likely you can't. But if you *think*, you can begin to see them as having it, and in doing so you can lose your fear of their attitude. You can also begin to mature at this point by quietly beginning to set your own more realistic standards. It wouldn't be totally impossible, you know, unless your parents are monsters, to have a sensible talk with them. Ask them if they don't feel that perhaps they are expecting too much of you? Or the wrong thing? At any rate, do some *thinking*.

Parents are people. They might even fool you and listen. Many of their motives may be hidden motives, even from themselves. But what can you lose by acting as mature as possible for you at this point, and at least offering them a hand in beginning to understand you as you are — not as they want you to be? If this kind of talk is possible, it will certainly have much more far reaching results if you approach them quietly and don't blow up. Let them in on the events of your life, both social and scholastic. They are hurt when you exclude them, you know, just as you are hurt when they exclude you. Ask their opinions now and then. Don't wait for them to force their opinions on you.

During the writing of this book, a provocative special supplement for college-age young people was published by the *Chicago Daily News.* Only outstanding, responsible, genuinely ambitious students were interviewed in one article which was headlined: "Parents, Keep Out! Students Say, Let Us Pick Our Own Careers."

I read the interviews carefully. In each one the student openly said: "Parents keep out!" or implied their gratitude that their parents had permitted them to choose for themselves. There was no bitterness in these quotations from young people entering college. But they were definite. I concur. Parents must guide, supply the money if possible, the encouragement, the transportation; but you as young people need the freedom to make your own choices where your life's work is concerned.

Does this sound somewhat lopsided, that parents should "supply the works" and leave the choice entirely up to you? Apparently it does, to some parents. The point I want to make here, though, is this: In most cases parents really love their young people. They care about you. They are not your enemies, your antagonists. They are your parents, and it isn't half as hard for them to do all that supplying as it is to let you leave their parental care. Don't resent them or feel uncomfortable if they weep a little when the train pulls out, or your plane takes off, or you slam the door of the driver's seat in your jalopy when it's time to go back to the campus.

Even though my mother always tried not to let me see her tears fall, for a long time I felt some kind of vague, uneasy guilt when she cried each time I left to go back to school. This was before I began to see her as another human being like myself. As soon as I did, I lost my vague guilt. I wasn't making her cry; she was shedding a few natural womanly tears because she would miss me. She wouldn't have had me stay at home for anything! She *loved* me. True love always concerns itself first with what is *best* for the loved one.

Give it a try. Put yourself as much as possible in your mother's place, or your father's. They are people like you, and they need you, and will need you in future years, maybe for a while, more than you will need them. Or more than you may *think* you need them. The glorious blend and balance comes, will come (*if* you have both tried to identify with each other) maybe many years from now, when they are old and you are older; then you will both know quietly that you need each other. It *can* come sooner, if someone begins now to *identify*. No one has ever aptly defined the strange, mysterious *need* for real communication between parents and children. It is needed not only for harmony in the home, it is needed in a way only God could have planted in everyone's heart.

If you're away at school, you know that everything in your day gets better if the letter from home tells you that all is well there.

This will not end when you have graduated from college or are settled in your own home. It will go on and on for the rest of your life, this deep-down desire to have things right at home. This does not indicate apron strings or silver cords; I believe it is God's doing. He put this desire for harmony among related human beings into our hearts. And because He is a dependable God, He is ready to supply you with the understanding you may lack where your parents are concerned. The years sometimes bring it, but why wait for that? God can give it to you now, any time you are ready to begin to cooperate with Him in learning how to *identify* with your parents.

12 *Finding Out About People*

If you have begun to think a bit more clearly about the tremendous potential of beginning to learn to identify with your parents, you are well on your way where *people* in general are concerned.

It is true that parents are people, but it is also true that all people are not parents. No matter how over-strict or possessive or unreasonable you may think your parents are, you will find other people generally far less willing to pacify you! Mom may have picked up your clothes and papers and gadgets where you dropped them at home, but with your first roommate (or second or third!) at school, this will, no doubt, be a sports car of a different color. At home the members of your family loved you just because you were you, even though tempers flared on occasion and you thought you couldn't wait to get away to college or into a job, where you would be appreciated.

I don't say you're not appreciated away from home, and I don't say you won't be. But as a general rule, outside your family circle you will be liked according to how much you deserve it. You won't be pampered, that's for sure. You won't be respected unless you've earned respect. If you're late coming into the girls' dorm some night, Mother won't be there to whisper, "I won't tell Daddy this time," and hurry you off to bed feeling loved anyway. The head of the dormitory will be there, and you will have to take your penalty, along with the others, with no one around to soften the blow for you.

Those of you who are already in college know this is true. You know, too, that campus life holds a brand new world of *people* to conquer. Everything is new about every person. Everything is new to them about you, too. It doesn't matter at all if your father was the leading doctor back in your home town. Oh, this would get you some respect if they knew it, but you're all too busy to find out about things like that for days and days. You are suddenly set down in a world full of new people, and the college student (or young person in the same new world of people in the office on that first job) had better start right out being interested in finding out about them.

An unusually beautiful young woman cried bitterly in my room at a summer retreat once, because she felt her whole first year at college had been an utter loss. After she stopped crying and began to speak realistically, instead of in super-dramatic parables, I got the true picture. In high school she had been the "most" — the most beautiful, the most popular, the most likely to succeed.

When she reached campus, she found twenty or thirty other girls equally as beautiful, equally as well dressed, and before the year was up, *more* popular than she was. High schools have a way of handing over to college campuses whole stacks of gals and fellows who held solo spots as the "most" back home. On campus, they either learn to "sing together" or you forget they're there.

Even this girl's disposition had gone bad on campus, even though, apparently, it had been reasonably attractive in high school. She hadn't thought this through at all; she was just sorry for herself, and somehow blamed college life in general. The truth was, of course, that things went so much her way at home that her disposition was never really seriously tried. In college, where she was just one of several hundred other young people, it *was* tried and found desperately wanting. She viewed her professors, her roommate, her classmates strictly from her vantage point. To her, everything revolved around *her*, and their treatment of *her*. Not to them, obviously, because as nearly as I could tell the people on campus were doing their best to forget she was around.

This pathetic-though-beautiful creature was finding out about people the hard way. Even those who had tried to make friends with her at first had given up by the end of the year. She was ensconced in a single room ("because I must have my privacy," she said), but it was obvious no one could get along with her in a double.

We have already said that it is characteristic of children to be *dependent*; it is characteristic of the young teen-ager to be *independent*. This girl clung stubbornly to both immature states, with no apparent desire whatever to begin the lifelong, interesting movement *away* from both *dependence* and *independence* into mature, balanced *interdependence*. Most of the

81

others at her school were moving on, but they were not willfully leaving her behind; she was just dragging her heels. She still wanted to be able to depend childishly on the adulation of other people whether she merited it or not, and like a cocky *young* teen-ager, she wanted to do it her way!

When we approach the twenties, and move out of the familiar safety zone of home and home town, we all find ourselves crashing head-on into the need for learning *interdependence*. That strange, ear-splitting sound you hear sometimes, when your problems crowd in between you and sleep at night, is not a gruesome thing, if you'll listen closely. It is life itself shouting to you, "Come on now, join the human race! Get in this thing with the rest of us. God created a human family — let's find out about each other and begin to live!"

One of the first things we need to find out about people is that they are, basically, like us. We all have particular idiosyncrasies, even eccentricities, individual talents and attractions (or lack of them); we are not all breath-takingly beautiful or handsome, but we are all *people*. And every other human being you know is just as eager for *acceptance* and *love* and *admiration* as you are. Some of us are more naturally fearful than others, some more courageous, some better humored, some basically more responsible. But deep down inside, the human heart is the same. The ancient Psalmist had caught on to this when he wrote: "The Lord has fashioned all our hearts *alike*."

Some students learn more quickly than others, some simply study more. But in varying degrees and with varying frequency, the person who sits next to you in class has the same quick nervousness inside, at least now and then, that you have when you're called on to recite. The other young person (older person, too!) who works in your office, if you are no longer in school, longs for the same words of commendation from the boss as you do. We all have the universal human weaknesses in common, and these can be marvelous starting points for learning to *identify* with each other.

I cannot stress too strongly, however, that recognizing another person's weakness must be followed immediately by a conscious moment of *caring* about that person. Otherwise, you can be a detriment to him or her. You can take advantage of that weakness, or you can use your sight of it to make you feel superior. True *understanding* means much more than a mere "catching on." True *understanding*, the only way to real *identification*, implies some action of concern directed *toward* the other person. It isn't enough to *see* someone else as he is; always, we must follow our seeing with *acceptance*.

What a tremendous thing it would be if you, at your age, could begin right now to act on the necessity to *accept other people as they are*. Think what this could eliminate by way of troublesome complications, not only in your life, but in the lives of all those people whom your life will touch on this earth.

One woman said to me many years ago that it took her twelve years to accept her husband *as he was*, because her sister had married such a wonderful man! Acceptance does not necessarily mean that we approve or condone. The poor woman's husband was a problem child at forty-one. He could not be approved, but finally she came to the place of *accepting* him without self-pity or envy of her sister, and almost at once God was able to get through to the man with some genuine improvement.

We make a great mistake when we confuse *acceptance* with *approval*. Can you see how much difference this could make in your attitudes toward other young people who do not know Jesus Christ, and whose behavior has, up to now, made you shun them? *Acceptance* does not mean *approval* and *participation*. Acceptance means you are expecting from that person only what that person is now able to deliver.

"I'm just at the point where I'm going to have to quit my job," a young woman of twenty-three wrote to me. "There is one girl in our office who is driving me into another world with her sloppy behavior and language. She seems to take it all out on me because I'm a Christian, and thinks that I'll just sit there like a lump and take it. She comes in late every other morning (usually with a hangover) and always I'm the one her boss calls for the dictation *she* should have taken. Do you think I should tell her off, or just up and quit?"

Here is a striking example of a Christian young person

83

who was just *not thinking clearly*. Granted, the girl was imposing on her, but since the letter went on for several more typewritten pages, I can tell you that what was irking her most was the fact that nothing *she* had said to this problem gal had changed her! She was *expecting* more of this girl than the girl could deliver. This does not imply approval, nor that she should be allowed to go on disrupting the office morning after morning. Still, when repeated warnings and near-threats had not changed her, my correspondent was puzzled. She was actually twirling *herself* up into a predicament by refusing to be realistic about her office situation.

Happily, I can tell you that the gal who wrote to me finally caught on and began to realize that she was expecting too much of an obviously deeply disturbed young woman who was without Christ. A real friendship resulted, and as I remember the correspondence, the last news was a show of real interest in Christianity from the once offensive friend. She had not *approved* her behavior, but she did come to *accept* her as she was.

Over and over I have heard women (old, and not so old) bemoan the fact that life somehow shouldn't treat them the way it does. In nine cases out of ten, one can soon discover that in the mix-up there is a lack of realistic *acceptance* somewhere. Only God can redeem, but we can clear the way by giving Him His first inroad into a needy life, through our realistic acceptance.

I know a man and woman, about my age, who are desperately trying to maneuver the wife's mother into a home for the aged, when in reality the mother can still care for herself and have her own home. True, she needs added attention from them, but they continue trying to force her to go. They already have the husband's mother living with them, and I can see that they just *can't help* being as they are. This is not to say they are right, but neither one knows God, and those of us who are trying to help untangle the sticky situation must *accept* these two as *being where they are right now* — apparently unable to cope with their lives.

"I have an English prof who really gives me a rough time because I'm a Christian. Don't get me wrong, I'm not blaming him. I understand his point of view. He was a preacher's kid and hates everything that has to do with church. Am I right to go out of my way to be nice to him? I don't try to convert him, the way some of the other Christian students have done, but I would surely love to see this man know God. They would make a marvelous team! I admire my prof. I am just going along, praying, of course, and trying to give that extra effort to his course."

This was a letter from a mature, wise, truly Christian young man. He does not expect more from his agnostic prof than the prof is capable of being right now. He has *accepted* him as he is, but it is *not* a passive acceptance. It has good, active prayer and love backing it up!

The kind of acceptance I am advocating does not imply "leaving well enough alone." It always carries motion in it, even though the activity may not show at first. There is no physical activity, don't forget, which can ever compare with the spiritual activity of real prayer.

You will also discover that you are finding out about people creatively when you begin to *give yourself to them.* You may read tomes on psychological understanding of the human personality. I am not attempting to enter the field of professional psychology in this chapter. But you will find the Christian practice of *acceptance* and *giving* substantiated by the authorities on human behavior.

God told us we were to love one another, and no one ever finds out about another person if love is absent. Only love's door is open to further discovery. And where there is real love, there has to be *giving.* If you truly understand this at your age, you are unusual. It just isn't usual for young people to grasp this truth in its widest sense. Few people ever practice it, even though they may have flashes of insight into

it. I am just beginning to observe its magnificent effects as I learn more and more each day to practice *giving love.* It always, always concerns itself first with the well-being of the other person. *Giving love* is always, always in motion *toward* the loved one. *Ordinary love,* the kind that concerns itself with the way the loved one is *making us feel,* says, "All right, I forgive you for what you did to me, now run along." *Giving love* says, "Yes, I forgive you, now come here!"

Giving love is, of course, God's kind of love. And those

of us who know Him personally know He never says, "run along" to anyone for any reason.

What does true *acceptance* and *giving love* really have to do with your life on campus? In the office or store where you work as a young person? Only everything. You, whether you know it or not, are affecting the people around you. You either make them comfortable or uncomfortable. If someone passes you on campus and doesn't speak or even smile, this you cannot help. But you *can* identify with the next person you meet by remembering the little chill that crept across your heart when you were snubbed.

Does this seem an over-simplification? Are you thinking, *What childish rot for a college student! We have more vital issues to think about.* Are there more vital issues than human relationships? We can only touch on them in this one chapter, but in all our complex twentieth-century world, is there a more vital issue than the people who live in our world? According to God, I believe not. He is deeply, incessantly interested in our economic situations, our forms of government, our national and social principles; but God is first of all interested in the *people* who live in His world. Jesus of Nazareth was first of all concerned with individual people. He did not come to set up the most powerful earthly Kingdom, as His followers then thought. He came to invade the individual hearts of every man, woman and young person. He is interested in our externals, but first of all, He seeks the human heart — the part of each one of us that longs for love and acceptance and security.

We tend to ignore, to push around, to deprecate those who annoy or fail to interest us. God, in Christ, always gives undivided attention, encouragement and confidence.

And He is always giving to everyone, with the concentrated interest of God Himself.

Can we do less than begin, at least, to *find out* about these people whom He loves so much?

13 Finding Out About Christian Conduct

Over and over again, by people of all ages, I have been asked what to me is an ambiguous question: How far can a Christian go?

This question in itself means little, but it is a dead give-away that the person who asks it has not stopped to think through the real issues involved in Christian conduct. As I see it, Christians are not primarily to be people who do a certain set of things, *nor* are they to be people who do *not* do another certain set of things.

Christians are people who have met God in Jesus Christ, and who have begun to take advantage of His power to live their lives in an orderly, sane, adequate manner. They have, by His grace, had their lives *returned* to the oneness with their Creator which He intended in the first place. The *eternal life* which Jesus Christ offers to us is a restoration of what Adam and Eve kicked away when they grabbed the reins of their lives into their own hands. It is not only some "sure road to heaven" at a dim future date. It is for *now*.

Anyone at any age who has received Jesus Christ into his human dilemma, has received God Himself. And with Him comes the same divine intelligence, sanity and balance which guided the earthly life of Jesus of Nazareth. He was the only true Son of God, but we are told in the Bible that even He "learned obedience." I doubt if anyone knows all that statement means, but if the Son Himself *learned*, should we demand pat answers and dodge the same process to which He submitted Himself?

Anyone who has received Jesus Christ as his Saviour has received the very wisdom of God Himself. Wisdom never functions within the confines of pat answers. Wisdom is active and operates not only according to God's nature, but according to the way things have been, according to the way things are, and according to the way they will be with us. God has always worked in the mainstream of human history, making use of what there was to use. Even His miracles made use of disease and suffering. He did not wipe out sickness; He *used* it. The wisdom of God (the only true wisdom) is

87

active. It can no more be shut up in a box of pat answers than God can be. If we attempt to confine the *living* subject of Christian conduct to a set of pat answers, we are simply being unrealistic.

"If I have the wisdom of God in me in Christ, why then don't I know always what's right and what's wrong?"

I think we *do* know more than we pretend, but one has only to take a few trips within even the circle of so-called conservative Christendom to see that there *is* an enormous amount of downright confusion. Especially among young people.

High-schoolers in particular try to pin one down on what's right and what's wrong. I have long ago lost count of how many young people (not only of high school age) have said: "My mother says it's okay if I go anywhere I'm sure I can take Jesus Christ with me."

What a statement! Think it through for a minute before you read further. Doesn't this imply that *we* decide where God is going? I can't help wondering what these well-meaning, but non-thinking, mothers really believe about God. Where do they think He will go, should their young people decide to spend an evening in a tavern, squandering their allowance on a 26 game? I am not being deliberately facetious. We must *think*. If a human being has found out anything about the God he follows, he will know that this God said specifically: "I will never leave you. . . ." If you spend an evening destroying yourself, God will be there fully conscious of you every minute!

Granted that we do have access to more wisdom from God than we make use of, He knew we would need some written guidance. God doesn't give pat answers, but He gives us all we need in the pages of the Bible, *if* we are thinking.

For the remainder of this chapter we are going to think about the tremendous potential in your life as a follower of Jesus Christ, *if* you will begin to think through four Scriptural checks for Christian conduct. They are all in the Bible, and there plainly. They are not listed in the index, because God wants us to *study* what He has said to us and then *learn* to apply it to our own daily rounds.

I have watched young people begin to do this, and I have followed these *four checks* in my own life for over a dozen years now. I can tell you, they work.

The *first check* is found in Colossians 3:17 — just the first part of the verse. This is what it says: "And whatsoever you do in word or deed, do (it) all in the Name of the Lord Jesus. . . ." What does His *Name* really mean? What does any name mean? Human beings can become accustomed to a name so comical it makes every stranger laugh. If we know the person, the person *defines* the name. When I was in high school, there were two shy little mountain gals who had come down to the city to do housework and attend our high school. Their names made us all laugh at first. Believe it or not, one was named Sweet Centers, and the other Arbutus Flowers! Sweet and Arbutus were inseparable. They had to be at first, anyway; we gave them such a rough time because of their clothes and their funny names. *But*, as the months went by, these plain mountain girls made us forget their peculiar names. They won us by their attractive dispositions and their steady, responsible behavior. Their *natures* defined their names.

Many men of Latin origin are named Jesus. But this One who came from God gave definition to His Name because of His *nature*. Is it not possible, then, to jot down our first check this way? *Can I do this thing, or be this way, or think these thoughts, and do it all in the nature of Jesus Christ? Would He do it?*

How many of your question marks does this eliminate where your Christian conduct is concerned?

The *second check* is found in the end of the same verse, Colossians 3:17: "And whatsoever you do in word or deed, do all . . . giving thanks to God and the Father by Him (Jesus)." How is this a check, when you feel like losing your temper or gossiping? How does giving thanks to God accomplish anything at that moment? Try it. The next time you tell a "small harmless white lie" say, "Thank You, Father, that I am so clever that I got by with that untruth." How do you feel about it? *Could* you do it? An old friend of mine broke his drinking habit, after his conversion, by *trying* to give thanks to the Father in the Name of the Son for every drink of bourbon! Of course, he couldn't do it. The bourbon was not only killing his chances of success, it was killing him, and God is never the giver of a "gift" like that.

"Thank You, Father, in the Name of Jesus, that I didn't get caught cheating on my math exam this morning."

"Thank You, Father, in the Name of Jesus, that I can be so casual about my carelessness."

"Thank You, Father, in the Name of Jesus, that I got by with what I got by with on that date last night."

I think you get the idea. So, a *workable* second check then would be: *Can I do this thing, or be this way or think these thoughts and thank God for it in the Name of Jesus? Can I give thanks for my conduct?*

The *third check* is found in 1 Corinthians 10:31: "Whether therefore you eat or drink or whatsoever you do, do (it) all to the glory of God."

Now, what does His *glory* mean? I once asked a group of small children this question, and received some imaginative and surprising answers. One little fellow with curly red hair said: "God's glory means the silver trumpets that play when He comes by." Another said: "God's glory is the big, yellow banner that waves at the head of His parade."

Were they entirely wrong? I think not. Both stunning definitions meant something that calls attention to God Himself. Both definitions had to do with the children's concept of Him. Of His *reputation* with them. Dr. Henry Drummond once defined God's glory as "His reputation." Certainly, where our lives are concerned in the area of conduct, this is true. So, is it far-fetched to read this verse this way? "Whether therefore you eat or drink, or whatsoever you do, do (it) all with the *reputation* of God in mind."

You and I, as His followers, do have His reputation in our hands wherever we go. We don't like the idea sometimes, but it's still true. If we are self-righteous, brittle, legal-minded "Christians," God Himself gets the blame for it. Most people have no strong concept of God whatever. Most people never read the Bible. But they do "read" us. And the fact remains that He dared to leave His reputation in the hands of mere human beings.

The *third check*, then, can go something like this: *Can I do these things, and be this way, and think these thoughts, and still be good for the reputation of the Lord I love? Is this going to help God's reputation with those who don't yet know Him?*

A young woman once said to me, "I'm actually afraid to become a Christian. I'm afraid I'll turn into a cross old worry-wart like my Grandmother! She's the only Christian I know, and if that's what God does to the human personality, let me stay away from Him."

Grandmother had been badgering the girl about her "life of sin," when she could have been *living* Jesus Christ before her. Do you blame the girl? I don't. Grandmother was no doubt sincere (whatever that means), but she was definitely *not* good for the reputation of Christ with her granddaughter.

Are you good for the reputation of the God who loves you so much?

The *fourth check* could be used alone — without any of the others, *if* you have really discovered God as He is. It is found in the Bible at the very end of the gospel of Matthew: ". . . lo, I am with you always." He is, you know, whether you're aware of it or not. God never reneges on a promise. He never forgets one. This word from Jesus Himself, just before He left our planet to go back to be with His Father and ours, seems sometimes so important to me, it is as though He were still saying — "Remember that, if you forget everything else." I believe it to be a uniquely important line to God, too. We always remember the last thing we read or hear most clearly, and He directed Matthew to end his gospel with these words: ". . . lo, I am with you always."

The fourth check must be clear to you already. *Can you do this thing, or be this way, or think these thoughts in His presence?* There is no way to get out of the presence of God. Have you ever thought about that? Think about it now. "I am with you always, even unto the end of the world." And then, because Jesus also said, "I am the beginning *and* the end," after this world, He will still *be*. We will be with Him, and He will be with us forever. Does this comfort you? Annoy you? Worry you? Leave you cold?

These words of Jesus, that He will never, never leave us, are much more than a check for outward forms of Christian conduct: They are either all of *life* to you, thorns in your flesh, or a matter of indifference.

If you are indifferent to them, it can mean only one thing: Regardless of the religion in your background, you

91

have simply not yet met Him in person. "*No man can see God* and live" in the same, old casual way again. When Jesus was on earth, people reacted strongly to Him. He divided them into two sharp groups: Those who followed Him because they came to believe in Him, and those who ultimately killed Him, or at least stood by and watched Him die. Whether *you* know Him or not, He knows you. And whether you are aware of His presence or not, He is everywhere, and that includes where you are, too.

Even if you are indifferent to Him, you may be sure that He is not indifferent to you.

If the knowledge that God is with you every minute of your life, whether He is welcome or not, makes you uneasy, resentful, fearful, you are much farther along the way than those who are indifferent. You at least recognize Him as God. You believe He meant what He said. Only you and God, of course, know *why* His presence makes you uneasy, and it is strictly between the two of you. The fact remains, He is there, and He will be there wherever you go and whatever you do all the way to the end of the world.

God is *there* for every man to reckon with, to learn about, to love, to follow or to reject.

But He is there.

Right there as you read this page now.

If His presence comforts you, delights you, stimulates you, you are an authentic Christian. I am never as impressed with what a man does or does not do, as I am with his attitude toward God. Many believers have the doctrine straight, according to their training, but never or seldom show any delight or interest in God Himself. He is here with me as I write to you, and He delights me. Not because I am a "good Christian," but because I am a Christian who has been unable *not* to go on finding out what He is like. The more we know about Jesus Christ, the more we rejoice that He will never leave us.

If His presence makes you uncomfortable, it could be that you are not guilty of any particular barrier-making between yourself and God. It could be that your concept of Him is so one-sided or twisted that the God you try to follow is just not the kind of God whose presence *could* fill

92

you with joy! Once more, let me urge you to discover Him *as He is* in Jesus Christ.

Then His presence will no longer seem to inhibit you. It will free you.

How far can a Christian go? What can a Christian do? *Anything he pleases, as long as he loves God.* Does this startle you? I hope it does. It is not original with me. St. Augustine said it first: "Love God, and then do as you please." Augustine did as he pleased *before* he loved God, so he was not speaking from a sheltered, fenced-in innocence or naiveté. *But* Jesus Christ so captured his heart that *after* his conversion he could still do as he pleased. *If* we have exposed our hearts to the Heart that broke on Calvary for us, we are *drawn* into the "bright captivity" of love. In this "bright captivity" we find ourselves *free* to live. It does not happen overnight that a man or woman loves God enough so that he or she will only want to please Him. But it can and does happen. This I believe to be His highest will for us. His heart holds no rule book, but it does hold us, if we permit it.

You can go on doing those things, being that way, thinking those thoughts, but you do not even think *alone*. There is no private corner where you can go and think your own thoughts. God knows. This is a fact, not a theory. Whether you believe it, or like it, is beside the point. He is there. He knows.

But He is not there to cramp your style, to restrain you, to keep you *from*. He is there to free you, to loose you, so you can always be going *toward* the abundant life. When Jesus spoke the words that raised His dear friend Lazarus from the dead, He made one telling comment: "Untie him, and give him a chance to move." This was totally characteristic of Jesus Christ. It still is. Always, in all ways, He is interested in your freedom to become all that you can become in Him.

External forms of conduct are not to be considered *first*. *You* are to be considered *first*, because *you* are first with God. If all is well with you both at the center of your being, if you are really following the living God, and not a religious idea of Him, you will find these four checks from His written Word sufficient. You will always *act* according to what you are becoming inside.

If you are allowing Him to love you into loving Him, as you *can* learn to love Him, you will find yourself moving toward the place where you will be able to love God and do as you please.

There is no delight on earth to compare with the free, open delight of the human heart when it is responding *naturally* to Jesus Christ.

The most creative and satisfying and joy-filled thing I know is to live so that we can look at Him, and be glad that He is looking back at us.

14 *Finding Out About Guilt*

"Most of the time I think I feel guilty just for being alive." The girl speaking twisted her handkerchief into a tight little knot and hung her head. "Every time one of my teachers calls on me in class, I am sure it is only because the instructor is positive I don't know the answer. Even if I do, I pile more guilt on myself because it always takes me so long to get it out."

This was a college junior, adequately intelligent, a hard worker who obviously, since she had reached her junior year, managed somehow to live at least far enough above her guilt to get by.

"Why do you think you feel so guilty?" I asked. "Do you have a theory?"

She raised her head, a little surprised at this. I think she expected a sermon on something like Christian courage. "Yes, I guess I do have a theory, but I didn't think I'd ever tell anyone. I guess I thought no one would be interested."

This young woman was a Christian, and I felt reasonably sure that her guilt was what would be normally called *false guilt*. She was not suffering from guilt before God as such, but she *was* suffering.

For one thing, she was not attractive looking. This alone can bring feelings of false guilt to a certain over-sensitive type of person. But her tense hands twisting that handkerchief without a pause convinced me that her looks caused only a part of her trouble. I am no psychologist, but I felt quite certain that her theory was the right one: At her mother's death, when the girl was ten years old, she had been sent to live with an aunt who had done a magnificent job of convincing her that no matter how hard she tried, nothing she ever did could be enough or right. "When I was sick with any of the childhood diseases I cried all the time because I was so ashamed that my aunt had to bring my food to me and take care of me. I felt guilty enough to die every time I caused her any trouble."

Most of us carry unnecessary *false guilt*. Those who love us and those who do not are equally capable of heaping it on us. I have learned the lesson of shedding false guilt the hard way since I have been a Christian. Somehow, because I write as I write and speak as I have spoken publicly for the last twelve years, a certain type of person gets the idea that I should manage to be available twenty-four hours of every day. If I get nervous, or show impatience, or am slower than usual in answering a letter, or have my once-a-week typist sign letters for me, my whole Christian concept is challenged by this particular type of individual. "I thought you were supposed to be a Christian. What happened to this great love you yak about? . . . etc., etc."

This is an old, familiar and exhausting story to anyone who attempts to circulate among human beings the Good News of God in Jesus Christ, by the printed page or in person. There will always be those whose self-centeredness is so complete that nothing anyone can do could possibly be more than a small down payment on what they think is due them. For years I tried to stop this by what I now see was harmful pampering. I hated the guilt they heaped on me and, since I have always felt that my critics *can* be the unpaid guardians of my soul, I took it seriously and tried to comply with their unreasonable demands on my time and energies. Slowly, God got through to me; and He did it by showing me the consequences of *false guilt* in the lives of other people. I saw the harm it did to their personalities, and gradually I began to reject it for myself.

If we are truthful, we must face the fact that parents, (frequently mothers) can be skillful at this business of heaping false guilt on their children's heads. "I go to church almost every Sunday, not because I want to go, but because I have to lie to my folks when I write home if I don't go. My mother, especially, has a sweet, almost charming way of making me feel so guilty if I don't." The young man who wrote this felt no guilt at not going to church; his guilt was *false* and his mother caused it. Instead of encouraging him to think through his need for a personal relationship with God for himself, she jostled him into the little rut of automatic church attendance, just so he wouldn't have to feel guilty with her.

Do you have a friend who heaps false guilt on you every time you are forced to break a date with him or her? Is there someone in your dorm or office or church who saddles you with sometimes unbearable personal obligation?

"Sometimes I enjoy walking home to my room from class alone," a liberal arts freshman told me once, "especially from English Lit class after we've had a really good session on some poem or book, and I'd like to have some time to think about it without talking to anyone. Do you think I can do this? Not unless I want to be made to feel like the world's worst heel all evening and far into the next day. There's a poor little gal who has a room in the same co-op house where I live, and if I don't wait for her after class she pouts for hours. I like her all right, but her world almost seems to revolve around me, and sometimes I feel terribly guilty about her — especially when I come right out and admit to myself that I wish she'd change schools, drop dead, or anything — just so I wouldn't have to feel guilty about her all the time!"

Think it through — always think it through when you have feelings which you recognize as guilt. *Have* you done something, willfully or unconsciously, to cause it? You alone, if you are in touch with the sensitizer of the human conscience, Jesus Christ, can know whether or not your conscience is clear and undeserving of guilt. He is the great sensitizer of your conscience, but He is, remember, *all sanity and balance*. You are only one person; at best you are a faulty human being, but God knows whether you have willfully done something to cause feelings of true guilt. *Check with Him*. If you feel clear, *act* clear. Let the touchy people go on heaping their false guilt upon you, but pay it no mind. Don't shake them off carelessly; sometimes broken relationships or frank talks are needed, but they can always be done in the Spirit, and with the definiteness of God Himself. If you are clear with Him, simply learn to ignore false guilt piled on your head by thoughtless, selfish and insensitive people.

Many, many young people carry loads of false guilt before God, too. Over and over I have heard them speak of their fear of doing something "He won't like." The full-to-overflowing Christian cup is not one that needs to be carried with tensed nerves for fear of spilling a drop! It is full to *overflowing* — the well of His Life is within you, "springing up to everlasting life." His idea for us is that we walk naturally, with our eyes on Him, not riveted on our precious cups which He is always filling for us.

There is, however, another kind of guilt that is not false — the guilt feelings we experience when we have willfully committed some sin or have wronged someone from selfish motives. If you cheated in that last final exam, you know it. You know that God knows it. You are guilty before Him and before the instructor, who may not even know it. This kind of guilt needs little explanation. It is familiar to us all. Here our sensitized consciences serve us well; but they can only serve us up to a point. If we have done wrong, our consciences tell us that we have, but from that point on they can do nothing but torment us. Here the Christian discovers one of his most-to-be-cherished freedoms: We *can* do something about it.

First of all, the Bible tells us that "if we confess our sins, He is faithful and just to forgive us. . . ." He is. It is as simple as that. I did not say it is easy, but it *is* simple. Just as surely as God is God, if you ask His forgiveness He will give it to you. There is no need for you to nourish worms in the fruit of your Christian life. The forgiveness of God cannot be explained fully in mere words, but it can be experienced fully by anyone at any time under any circumstances. The forgiveness of God is not a theory, it is a fact. It is not passive, it is *active*. It is far more than a pardon. He says to us, in effect: "You're forgiven, your slate is clean — now, let Me help you, with all My energy, to stay clean." He forgives us, then He gets right into things with us — not just to see that we don't "cross Him" again, but to do all in His power to see that the same harmful thing does not strike us, His loved ones, a second or a third time.

Young people cheat on exams, steal money, commit adultery, tell big and little lies, and break laws. So do adults. We adults have no exams, but we do have income tax forms to fill out, and cheating is cheating. If you have sinned against God in any of the above categories, this is certainly no news to you. But young people as well as adults also gossip (steal reputations), break up friendships, appear more pious than they really are, "create" engagements to get out of undesirable ones, and decide who's Christian and who's not. If you were falling on your knees to worship a silver statue, you would recognize at once that you were sinning against the Lord God. You would call it idolatry. What about the Christians (young and old) who worship their denominations or their leaders to the actual harm and exclusion of those who don't agree with them? Some young people (because adults have taught them) seem actually to worship the Bible, rather than the God of the Bible. Does this shock you? Think it through.

I was speaking one night on John 3:16. I knew it from memory and did not need to read it from a bound book. I walked onto the platform of the church where I was speaking and left my Bible in the pew with my purse and coat. After the service was over a man informed me that if I did not feel I needed to carry the Word of God with me and read from it, they did not need me to speak in their church. This to me is Bible worship, and it is another form of idolatry.

The nature of our sin against God is beside the point, however. God is just as willing to forgive that misguided brother as He was to forgive me for the reaction I had against him. In fact, after that night, I have found it much simpler to *understand* that all Christians have areas that are still dark. God forgave me because I really wanted forgiveness and He had promised it. But then, as always, I found His forgiveness to be *active*. I was not only pardoned, I was *added to* at the center of my being.

Guilt feelings that result from some conscious act or thought on our part are the warnings from God that we need to seek forgiveness. To carry around our guilt feelings *after* we have received this forgiveness, however, is an insult to the One who hung on His cross to prove His heart to us once and for all! It is natural for young people to be introspective, but don't let your youth betray you here. Without realizing it, sometimes we continue to flail ourselves because it smacks of the dramatic. We all love dramatic, important thoughts about ourselves. Don't cultivate this. Don't retard your maturity. When you find older people still clinging dramatically to guilt or confusion after what God has done for them, make a quiet note that they are still immature persons and don't expect them to *act* like adults until they have matured a lot more.

When He forgives us, He puts our transgression out of His mind, so why shouldn't we do the same? Some unhealthy minds seem unable to do this, but I am not writing to those in need of mental help. I am writing to you, with your normal mind, and appealing to you to use it. If He said He would forget your transgression as though it had been dropped into the deepest sea, believe Him. He has put your transgression as far from you as the east is from the west; why cling to something that is just not there?

There is, of course, the *universal guilt* shared by all mankind — even by those who have not found out about it yet. This can or cannot cause recognizable guilt feelings. The self-development cults propagate the mental exercise of denying guilt, and psychologically this gives temporary peace of mind.

The fact remains that the Bible tells us, and the Christian faith holds, that we are all born *guilty* in the eyes of God, since we are all born into the human race, and man at one point jerked himself loose from the loving control of His Creator. This is not a pretty thought; in fact, it is rejected by more people than accept it, because it staggers the human concept of *justice*.

"How do you expect me to follow the kind of God who would hold *me* as guilty for something a fellow named Adam did in some legendary old garden I don't even believe existed!"

The good-looking young man who snarled this question at me one night in a seminar on his campus, lost his poise completely before he finished his sentence. Up to that point, he had been in full command of his every objection to what I had said earlier. Why did he go to pieces on that one? His handsome face reddened with anger and humiliation, but I think it was more than that. I think his heart squeezed a little within him before he got it out. The point here is not whether or not he believed in Adam and Eve in their garden. The point here is that something within him was witnessing to the *truth* of what he was trying to tear down.

I find no trouble accepting the truth in the Genesis account of man's severance from God. The trouble came for me when I faced the fact that, simply because I had found myself helpless against certain forces in my own nature, I was being rushed by Love Himself to the place of confessing my own *need* for the first time in my life!

Far be it from me to argue the Adam and Eve story with anyone here; but I *know* the truth contained in it. And anyone who takes even a quick peek around at our world can know it, if he is honest. Would anyone, by the wildest stretch of the most elastic imagination, ever think that man, if he had not jerked himself loose from God, would have engineered the world into its present chaotic condition? If man in his human nature, developed to its highest capacity, is enough, why are things in the mess they're in? Our forefathers, if they could have seen into the commonplace of today, would have believed it to be "miracle." Compared to the way they lived, "we have it made." But has human nature changed? Basically, not at all. Man is still, with all his progress, in the same helpless dilemma. And human nature does not change until it relinks itself with the life of the same Creator who thought it up in the first place.

To say we are all *guilty* before God, until we have been reunited with Him through faith in Jesus Christ, is so much "bilge" to the non-Christian. But has anyone come up with a better way? For that matter, has anyone come up with *another* way? We are *not* guilty in the sense that we should cringe before Him. It was not Jesus' way to point His finger at a man and shout: "Shame on you, you filthy sinner!" I am told that some preachers employ this strange method, but I am a Christian, and that means I take only Jesus Christ's thinking as *absolute*. He did not do this. He spoke of the weariness, the burdens, the sickness of sin in the lives of His loved ones. Mile after weary mile He pushed His human energies to the breaking point in order to show the whole world — Pharisee, Jew, Roman, disciple alike — that God can never run out of love for His creatures. He healed and blessed and lifted. He did *not* condemn. "The Son of Man came, *not* to condemn, but to save," Jesus said, and again and again He demonstrated it by His every action.

It is not that God intends that this universal guilt should drive us to our knees in shame and self-hatred; rather, that we should look at Him, as He really showed Himself to be in Jesus, and fall gratefully to our knees in repentance and joy that God's love *could* not let us go.

This third kind of guilt, the kind common to every man,

need leave no one in despair. When we realize our part in it, we can begin to rejoice! It is then that we can be returned to the Father, through His Son. This third kind of guilt, as I see it, is not the same *from our side*, as the second kind, where we know we willingly sinned. This universal guilt is to be recognized as a disease common to every man, but from which every man can be healed.

God is not angry with *you* because Adam did what he did. God is eternally concerned that you be set free from your unhappy inheritance.

If we could get it straight, once and for all, that *everything* about God is redemptive — geared to lift us, to recreate, *never* to smash down or destroy, what a different people would inhabit the earth He gave us.

I do not understand God's *justice* as being tempered by what we deserve or do not deserve. I don't think this enters into it. I simply do not understand God's justice at all. It is far too much for me. It is not merely higher than human justice as we understand it. How could it be a justice only *different in degree* from even the highest human concept of justice? It must be a justice totally *different in kind*. This eliminates the well-worn complaint about God's justice in holding all humanity guilty for what one man did. It forces us to the realistic acceptance of the fact that *if* His justice could be compared favorably or unfavorably with ours, the logical conclusion would have to be that, since He is a just God, almost no one would ever be returned to harmony with Himself. If He acted on the principles on which our highest human courts act, who among us would be *deserving* of the freedom He offers to everyone?

As things are, we dare not think of guilt without simultaneously thinking of His Love. God knows this, and that is why no man ever really gets a clear picture of his need of a Saviour *until* he gets a clear picture of the Saviour Himself. No man could bear it. Every man would break under it.

On His cross God Himself, in the Person of Jesus Christ, stretched out His arms toward the whole weary, burdened, sin-twisted world — in love. Not in judgment. Not in condemnation. Not to make us ashamed, but to give us a clear picture of our need at the same moment He gives the clear picture of His supply for that need.

To me, Jesus on His cross is God Himself crying to every person in your town, on your campus, in my town — in the whole tormented world: "Look at Me. This is what I'm really like! Look at Me. I'm *giving* Myself to *you*. This is the way I love you — like this, with My arms stretched out and My heart exposed — to you. I and the Father are one, and *this* is the way you are loved. This is the only way I can love. Now, give Me your guilt; I've brought you My peace to replace it."

15 *Finding Out About Fear*

It appears to me that the more man discovers about the universe, the more basis there is for the universal fear of the unknown. I went to college during the years when, on most campuses, *science* was man's god. "Man has little or no need for religion now," I remember one professor saying. "The ancients had need of a god behind every bush and in every sunrise. Now modern man has discovered enough about the universe so that he needs no gods to placate his superstitious fears."

Without a doubt, education has laid to rest the bogeyman of superstition, but our knowledge has increased to the extreme where once more the old haunting fear and need are returning to man's mind and heart. The more we learn, the more we realize we do not know. The fear and the emptiness are once more recognizable to anyone who thinks. This same professor also doubted that the atom would be split in our century. He was not a backward gent. This was simply thirty years ago. And, indeed, it was a reasonably comfortable period, not predominated by fear. You see, *yours* is the first generation to have been born and forced to live daily lives with the knowledge that man could, at any moment, destroy civilization. There was no such thing as nuclear neurosis when I was your age — no big, outward reason to be afraid. So, the seemingly shallow observations of my chemistry prof were not as "far out" as they seem now. I grew up *between* world wars. With all my heart, I hope this is not true with you, too. But even though I was comparatively young when World War II was declared, it was only toward the end of that war that Hiroshima happened. Wars when I was your age were still considered, at least by the average person, to be the sole business of the military.

Yours is a generation with a totally new and totally understandable reason for *fear*.

I do not mean merely the fear of nuclear invasion. I speak of the nameless fear haunting the deepest pocket of mankind's heart: the fear of our seeming helplessness. *Is there nothing anyone can do about us down here?*

We read news coverages of round-table discussions

among the world's leading nuclear scientists, and we quake to hear them call for some kind of braking measure. "Man's rapidly increasing knowledge of the unleashed power of the universe can destroy him," they repeat. And our hearts squeeze with the nameless *fear*. *Who* can apply the brakes? *Are* there any? Oh, we go on about our work and our daily lives; we plan careers and marriages and new industries; we make new laws and introduce new bills in government; we go out to dinner and buy our favorite records and books. But with us always is the *fear*.

Here we must stop a moment to remind ourselves that there *are* two kinds of fear, healthy and unhealthy. This is not a new thought, but it is a steadying thing to remember. The surgeon must keep his healthy fear of carelessness with his scalpel in his hand; behind the wheel of an automobile, healthy fear is necessary; statesmen must remember to fear the possible outcome of hasty action. All this is merely essential *respect* for danger. This kind of healthy fear is the valued possession of any maturing individual. If we are to live constructive lives, we must keep it well in mind.

We need to find out about healthy fear and make use of it.

But we also need to find out about unhealthy fear, the kind of fear Franklin Roosevelt meant when he said at the outbreak of World War II, "We have nothing to fear but fear itself." Unhealthy fear is as deadly to the human personality as a malignant cancer to the body. Jesus said, "The kingdom is within you." It is. God created us for peaceful living, in mentally and physically healthy surroundings. We have twisted His original plan and we pay the penalty in *fear*. No need to pursue medical statistics here. Human beings *can* be literally frightened to death. Several years ago I remember reading a newspaper account of a butcher accidentally locked in his meat storage room overnight. He was found the next morning, dead. And on the wall of the room he had scrawled, "I am freezing to death." The temperature of the room was 36 degrees; he died of fright.

The story has been repeated millions of times. It will go on being repeated, because uncontrolled fear will remain as long as man orbits independently of God.

Does this imply that those who believe in God have no
105

uncontrolled, unhealthy fears? Does it imply that fear is uncontrollable without God? Does it imply that godless men lack courage? We have attempted to be realistic in this book so far, and nothing would be gained by a departure from reality now. Men do demonstrate great courage without a knowledge of the living God. But the kind of gnawing, unhealthy fear we speak of is seldom if ever overcome by a show of human courage. It is buried by it, or pushed to one side temporarily, but not overcome.

Your generation is the first to be born into the potential danger of nuclear holocaust, but I dare to believe that the threat of nuclear destruction is only an *intensifier* of the age-old fear that has haunted man's heart through all the centuries since he jerked himself loose from the control of his Creator. Man under God's control is also under God's care. This in no way means that believers in the Lord God are going to be made "cosmic pets" of the Father, immune to hardship and tragedy. Christians are not immune to unhealthy fear. But only Christians can be freed from it, once they have faced it and remembered what their God is really like.

In the Bible we are told that "perfect love casts out fear." What does this really mean? It seems to me that, once and for all, we should rid ourselves of the idea that this is a pat formula for never being afraid again. It is also far past the time for Christians (not caught for the moment in a web of destructive fear) to stop using this verse as a kind of spiritual dare or threat to those who happen to be suffering from fear.

"Now, don't quote that verse at me about 'perfect love casting out fear,' because I'm sick and tired of so-called victorious Christians trying to make me feel like a heel just because I'm afraid!" The young woman who began a talk with me on that note struck a deeper note than she realized. She had a genuine reason for her fear, and apparently some well-meaning friends had tried to help her with this magnificent verse. But to my mind, it is generally interpreted *backwards*. If we are fearful, we are made to feel that somehow *our* love for God is imperfect or we wouldn't be afraid.

Formula religion like this not only bores me, it strikes *fear* in me. The kind of healthy fear I have come to respect.

Like the surgeon who must fear a slip of his hand that holds the scalpel, we who speak of God's answer for the dilemmas of human existence must also fear carelessness when we quote from God's written Word. To me, the "perfect love" that dispels fear is not our love, but *God's*. This should be obvious. It is, if we are thinking realistically. Do you know a single human being with perfect love? This young woman and I had an interesting discussion of the verse she brought up. "Well, maybe it doesn't mean *my* love is supposed to be perfect — but they at least make me feel as though something must be wrong with *my response* to God's love. Anyway, every time I talk to a Christian I just get guilt heaped on top of my fear because they always quote that verse."

This girl was not a mentally disturbed person. She had gotten herself into trouble with the authorities, and her fear of the outcome was normal. There was reason for it. Where were her friends wrong in their emphasis? Isn't it true that "perfect love casts out fear"? Yes, it's true. But no magic formula is concealed in the verse. It is, like all the rest of the Bible, *not* static, but dynamic. Within these words is all power to overcome fear of any kind, but the words themselves are not magical. Neither is the God whose love *is* perfect. He is *life*, and He moves realistically within the stream of human history, in each individual life history and in the history of nations. For this verse to have constructive, useful meaning to you, it is first essential for you to know enough about this God whose love is perfect. For any verse from the Bible to have useful meaning, this is necessary.

During the terrible weeks while my father lay dying of leukemia, I found myself being caught up in a growing state of fear. Grief and anxiety and heartbreak are normal at a time like that, but when fear is added to the load it becomes unbearable. We knew medical science had run out of hope in his case. I had made a definite transaction with God in which I *gave* my beloved Dad to Jesus Christ — as true a relinquishment as I know how to make. I did not fear his death (he knew God intimately), but I feared life without him. What would my mother do? How could I face her grief along with my brother's and my own? Soon I even lost sight of the actual reasons for my fear and sank into *fear* itself, destructive fear. *But* this fear lasted only as long as I gave it my attention. What gets your attention, gets you. As soon as I deliberately put my attention back onto the nature of Jesus Christ, and began to act on the *fact* that He was in charge of the future too, my fear of it vanished like an April snowflake. Dad's condition did not change, but I did. Why? Was it because of *my* perfect love toward God? Of course not. My love toward God isn't perfect. Was it because of my superior response to God's love? No. *It was because of God Himself.* I don't think He even cast out the fear. I think He just went on being Himself, and as soon as my attention riveted itself on Him, the fear could not stay around.

This involved no particular spiritual exercise or talent on my part whatever. The only positives I brought to the situation were my years spent in discovering Him as He revealed Himself to be in Jesus Christ, and my willingness to stop agitating and begin to act as though I believed my discoveries about Him. I did *not* begin to believe that He wouldn't allow something so terrible to happen to me, His chosen one. Life hands ghastly blows to God's people every day. I merely began to act on what I had already come to believe about Jesus Christ Himself. And that is that, no matter what happens, He, because He *is* the Redeemer, will not allow it to be wasted. He could not be Himself without being redemptive in all things. He could not be Himself without *being* love.

Fear drives otherwise adequate people to drastic ends. I doubt that any psychiatrist would disagree that fear lies at the basis of most mental disturbances. I am no authority here, but I have watched people of all ages destroying themselves and their families and friends because they simply did not know how to cope with their fears. There is no final way for *us* to cope with them permanently, but we can learn enough about the nature of God Himself until one day we are enabled to turn our first attentions on Him.

Where Jesus is, fear cannot survive. He is God. "God is love," and perfect love does cast out fear.

There is no formula involved here. Faith is involved. Not faith alone (I doubt if there is such a thing!), but an active, daring faith *in the nature* of the God who hung uncomplainingly on His cross to reveal Himself as love: the kind of love that *can* cast out fear.

Just as God is never the author of confusion, so He is never the author of fear. Paul wrote two important letters to a young man named Timothy, who meant a great deal to the old apostle — letters so important to us they became a part of our Bible. Near the beginning of the second of these letters, Paul wrote: ". . . God hath not given us the spirit of fear; but of power and of love and of a sound mind." If you are afraid, and if the fear lingers, you may be sure it does not come from God. Can you imagine God's Spirit being afraid? Can you?

What held Jesus of Nazareth steady and poised, able to be silent, before Pilate? Was it His supreme human courage? True, in Jesus, God did become a human being, but He also remained God, and it was God's Spirit which held Him during those fearful moments before the Roman who — for the duration of Jesus' earthly life, at any rate — held His fate in his hands. You may argue: "But Jesus knew His Father could have sent enough angels to save Him. I don't know *what's* going to happen to *me* if my worst fears materialize." True. But Jesus had it straight in His mind about the Father's will. Gethsemane was past when He stood before Pilate. There was no trick of intellect involved on Jesus' part; no declaring His fear away; He had no fear. Dread, surely, but no fear. God's Spirit knows no fear.

Has God given us a spirit *other* than His own? Was Paul wrong when he wrote to young Timothy that God had *not* given him the spirit of fear?

Is God's perfect love involved in His Spirit? It has to be! God *is* love. Love isn't just one of His many characteristics. The Bible tells us He *is* love. Could His Spirit, then, plant willy-nilly within us seeds of something which God does not possess?

Granted that all mankind experiences an understandable fear for the state of the world in the twentieth century; but if this fear is healthy, that is, not based on cowardice, we need not be ashamed of it. The Berkeley Bible translates Paul's line from his letter to Timothy this way: ". . . God has not given us a spirit of cowardice, but of power and love and self-control." Are these, then, God's definitions of what lies on the *opposite* side of destructive fear?

Examine the word, *power*, where it might pertain to your own daily life. Eliminate all ideas of the use of this word as a means to get your own way; forget the expression "power-crazy." Examine it in the sense that we, as human beings, need *power* in order to live constructive lives. What do you find? Have you experienced inner power at a particular moment when you were able *not* to defend yourself in an argument? Have you experienced the stimulation of real power of concentration? Of power to resist temptation? Was fear connected in any way with these experiences of *power* within you? No, it could not be. Fear forces us to self-defense, to worry; and "worry," as someone once said, "is a cycle of inefficient thought whirling about a center of *fear*." Worry causes increased fear, just as surely as fear can cause increased worry. A cycle results, and inefficiency. This is illustrated at its simplest when you are trying to concentrate in your study for an important exam, and your *fear* negates your normal power of concentration.

Paul wrote to Timothy that God had not given the spirit of fear, but of *power*. So, power is surely one of fear's opposites. The apostle also told his young friend that God had given him the spirit of *love*, not fear. Real love, as we see it in Jesus Christ, is out-going, seeking for places to give itself away. Fear shuts us up behind walls of self-concern. People who are filled with fear seldom give a thought to anything but their fear. If anyone else is involved at all, it is, to them, in direct relation to their fear.

Most of us, I think, would agree that we *fear people* and their opinions or their actions more than we fear the possibility of nuclear war! If we fear people, how can we love them? Fear turns us in toward *us*. If we size up the human race around us according to how its members are treating us or making us feel, we are, in reality, only thinking about ourselves. Can love be involved here?

"I try to make friends," a young man told me recently, "but every time I walk across the office where I work I'm just scared to death of all the people watching me from behind their desks. I know they don't like me, and I'm so afraid of them I freeze when I have a chance to talk."

In the first place, the other people in his office probably

were not watching him. But he was so full of fear of these people he was unable to believe anything else. The boy admitted he had never tried to concentrate on the people as human beings like himself, struggling with their own fears and problems. "I guess I figured since they seem to get along with each other, they couldn't be like me."

Love gives itself away. Fear locks its doors, and then blames other people for not breaking in!

The young man Timothy never got sounder advice from his old friend Paul. God does *not* give us the spirit of fear. In its place He gives the spirit of power and love, both characteristic of His own heart. Both demonstrated in Jesus Christ. Paul did not stop there, however, but assured Timothy that, along with power and love, God had also given the spirit of "a sound mind."

For our purposes, we will not consider a "sound mind" as opposed to a mentally unsound one. This is not a book about mentally disturbed young people. I would have no basis or authority for writing such a book. In examining this last *opposite* of fear, which Paul mentioned in his second letter to Timothy, the Berkeley translation is apt: ". . . God has not given us the spirit of cowardice, but of . . . *self-control*."

Self-control is so obviously the opposite of fear that it requires little explanation. Here again, as with *power* and *love*, Jesus of Nazareth is the most striking demonstration of self-control. By the wildest stretch of anyone's imagination, could a *fearful* person be thought of as *self-controlled?* The two states simply cannot exist together. While most young women scream when they're suddenly fearful, and while most young men do not — their *self-control* comes out about the same, I'm sure. But composure, self-control, does not vanish only in the presence of sudden, startling fears. Daily, nagging fear scatters our poise and self-control in an even more devastating way. Sudden fears often pass as suddenly as they come; inner fears do not. A quick rise in blood pressure from some sudden fright brings a quick tensing of our conscious behavior. But anything that is sudden and cataclysmic is easier to control or to dispense with than the deep-down hidden disturbance. Deep-down fears build daily tension — today's on top of what was already there from yesterday, and self-control is impossible.

I am convinced that much of the so-called questionable conduct of young people is due to such deep-down, half-hidden fear and tension. Adults analyze you and call you *immoral* or, at best, *amoral.* You are classified as *conformists, rebels, nonconformists.* Not being an educator, I choose to read these tomes written about you, and then do my own thinking. And I see you as people. *Young* people. I see no need to criticize you, *or* fly to your defense. I am more interested in *understanding* you, from your vantage point, not mine. And I believe with all my heart that an enormous amount of the much-condemned and much-analyzed behavior of young people stems from your various inadequate methods of handling your fears.

Some of you are *egoists:* the age-old method of covering up fear and inadequacy. Some of you are *rebels:* also an ancient (though no more successful) method of protesting against the state of things — things that make you afraid. Some of you are *nonconformists:* another way (highly familiar to me) of "handling" fear (in this case, fear of being like other people who bore or frighten you). Some of you are *conformists;* in one way, this is the most difficult and most unrealistic method of handling fear. It seems the simplest when you are young; much easier, you reason, to do it the way you're told to do it and thereby gain approval. You fear being different, fear displeasing your teachers, your parents, your friends. The conformist, however, is cruel to his or her real self. The conformist necessarily cannot do much realistic thinking.

None of these ways works toward a successful, fulfilling life, but they are the usual methods of attempting to handle that basic uneasiness, that nagging inner fear. At best, they only keep the fear shoved down into the subconscious mind. Eventually, except perhaps with the extreme conformists, the lid blows off for one reason or another, and there it is again.

You are not all rigidly in one of these classifications. This, of course, is one reason I object to such rigidly drawn lines. You *are* people, and people created in God's image should avoid methods to cope with their lives which cause their personalities to become so easily classified. You have the glorious, God-given right and obligation to *find out for yourself* about *yourself*. If you are afraid in one certain area of your life, one Person already knows it, so why waste your good energies trying to pretend the fear is nonexistent? Why work so hard at fooling *people* that you eventually fool yourself? I do believe that refusal to face our fears causes much of our destructive conduct — at your age and at mine.

Face that fear, no matter what it is, but be sure you face it *conscious* that you are doing it in the all-caring, all-understanding presence of Jesus Christ, who is interested with every ounce of His energy in seeing you free of it. He does not want your personality distorted by fear. He does not want your thinking or your moral judgment warped by it. And as powerful as that fear is, it *cannot* remain in your mind as long as your mind is on Him!

"I'm afraid of what I've just discovered about myself," a university sophomore confessed. "I've just found out that I'm afraid of too much knowledge. Now I've got still another fear. There's so much to learn all of a sudden, I'm afraid. How do I know what is safe to learn?"

Once education was based on a handful of truths — absolutes. Now ideas seem to change with every new scientific discovery, with every new school of literature or philosophy. If you share that fear of "too much to learn," it is understandable. I do not advocate a return to old methods of education. This is not our point here. I do urge you, however, to consider that there is still one Absolute available to everyone: God. He may be taught as a marginal issue, but this does not mean that He is. He is still God. Jesus Christ's visit to our earth has exactly the same impact today as it had when He came, and that impact was the same as it was "in the beginning."

Our world changes so rapidly, *fear* is the inevitable consequence. But "Jesus Christ (is) the same yesterday, today and forever." If, as Christians believe, He is God, then all of us can begin our search for fulfillment with one unchanging and unchangeable Absolute. If you know *where* you are going, the shadows are not so large, nor the rocks in the road so apt to make you stumble. If you are just *going*, hoping for the best, fear walks with you every step of the way.

The God of Calvary despises *emptiness* in you, as nature
113

abhors a vacuum. He knows that where there is *emptiness*, fear rushes in, just as air rushes into any available space. If your habit is to think and think and think about your fear, or the reasons for your fear, consider this: You control your conscious mind, don't you? We don't have control over our subconscious minds, except to govern what we drop down into them, but we can have mastery over our conscious minds. Why not try an experiment for a set period of time — say, one month? Every time your fear gets your attention, make a definite act of turning your attention directly onto the Person of Jesus Christ. If you have to sing to Him, quote some verse from the Bible, form the words of a prayer, look at a picture of Him — whatever is needed to get your attention onto Jesus, Himself, do it. When you sit down in a lecture room, you turn your attention on the professor, or, at least, this is usually advisable. Do the same thing with Christ, *every* time fear takes over in you for any reason. What you do upwards of thirty times becomes a habit with you. We are all capable of forming good habits as well as bad ones.

Don't wait until you "feel" God's presence. Maybe you didn't get enough sleep last night, and your emotions are out of tune. Turn your attention on Him deliberately, by an act of your conscious mind, no matter how you feel. There's never any need to wait for Him to arrive. He's there, every minute of every day for all the rest of your life — whether you know Him or not. And He is profoundly acquainted with *you*. There will be no need to explain yourself or your fears to Him. He already knows all there is to know about you.

And I can promise you — not because of what I know about you, but because of what I know about Him — that if you recognize Him, and open yourself and your inner emptiness to His Spirit, you will find the "spirit of fear" making a quick exit.

16 Finding Out About Your Real Potential

In my mail this morning came a letter from my mother, which seems to give me an apt beginning for this last chapter. Mother tells me of a visit from a well-to-do woman whose attractive, intelligent daughter is a junior in one of the country's leading universities. "All of her daughter's friends on campus are from similar backgrounds," Mother wrote. "They are all from well-to-do families, and from babyhood they have had every possible opportunity to reach their highest potential in life. But my friend says that psycho-analysis is the latest fad on campus! Practically everyone who can afford it is being analyzed."

What does this mean? Does it mean these young people are sick? Actually in need of analysis? Are they merely bored? Does it mean that they are in this restless state *only* because they are *not* Christian believers? I have no way of knowing what they believe; and the actual *need* for a psychiatrist is not really our point here, anyway. This must be individually discovered, but where there is a "fad" in operation, we should be able to draw some conclusions.

Is it necessarily a tragic and unhealthy sign that these students are flocking to psychiatrists? I think not. It is not so unhealthy as it is unnecessary. And yet, we oldsters dare not throw up our hands and click our tongues over it. We have handed young people a world in which their present emptiness has been cultivated. These students who are going in for analysis are the inevitable products of a mainly *materialistic* society. They wear stunning clothes, the latest hairdos, attend the best schools, drive their own cars, all with full financial backing by their parents. Their parents are educated, intelligent people. But the *inner beings* of these young people wander, like trim little vessels, equipped with all the necessary accoutrement for a successful voyage, *except* a rudder.

They will graduate into a ready-made career, most likely assured of financial success. They know this. They have always had the "right connections." Is this wrong? Not at all. It is a good thing, but it is just not enough. As I write this, young people are swarming to campus bookstores to buy the books of J. D. Salinger and William Golding. Excellent taste in writing. (We are not discussing the pros and cons of censorship, or the need for it, here.) But I believe students have boosted the royalties of these capable writers because their books depict the strange, wandering pursuit of the young. If you are a Salinger or a Golding devoteé, do not think I am your adversary. These men are writing realistically — about most people as they are. To me, much contemporary literature, especially Salinger, rather describes a current trend, creating, as Mary McCarthy says, "a kind of phony religiosity" among young people, making no pretense at offering a solution. This is good, so far as it goes. It can, in the true thinkers among you, propel you toward a deeper search for truth. But it is tragedy when anyone, young or old, does not pursue truth *beyond what can be experienced with the senses.* Unless a young person is exposed to the possible potential of his own life through an exposure to the "something beyond" himself and his experience, the God-planted desire for discovery dies out. When it goes, it is replaced by the vague, restless uneasiness which haunts our century.

I see these students and their "fad" for analysis as human beings still searching for God. In the main, *they do not know this.* They would perhaps laugh, or look puzzled, or argue the issue. But there is no escaping the fact that the "Lord (has) fashioned our hearts alike." Hearts are not limited to emotion. I make no plea for a mere religious emotional bath, refreshing as that can be for a time. The movement must be toward *reality*, permanent seeing, decisive involvement of the will.

One of America's great writers, the late Ernest Hemingway, preached a religion of *nada*, nihilism, nothingness. This is what he saw and believed, and few have ever communicated with such strength and beauty of language. But has his *nada* been enough? "Our father, who art in *nada*, hallowed be thy *nada*."

Hemingway saw deeply into the tremendous potential of *human* nature, but with all the courage he both possessed and wrote about, it was not enough. *Nada* is not man's native climate. We face the facts when we begin to see that man was created for full *being*, to reach his highest *potential in*

God, now — on this earth. If God created for nothingness, He is nothing Himself. No writer has communicated the high, *human* potential of man as did Hemingway, but it was not enough. No wonder his own courageous heart gave up at last. It had been fashioned, too, by the God who, to him, was *nada.* His heart could not face nothingness anymore than yours or mine. This great man of letters is to be admired for his work, and *understood* for the hunger in his heart, not condemned.

The students who are "going in" for psychoanalysis are to be understood for the hunger in their hearts, not condemned, not deprecated. The human heart struggles with the two questions common to us all: Why am I here? Where am I going? Only the superficial among us will deny this, or fail to recognize the questioning, either within himself or within the heart of his fellow man. Only the superficial among us would label the honest admission of these questions as weakness or ingratitude. To question our existence and our future potential is only human. I believe God counts on our asking these questions. He counts on the basic unrest they create in us; He knows that without them we will never reach beyond ourselves.

These students are seeking an answer. To me their fad, while it is likely to end in still more confusion, is at least hopeful. Only when the human heart stops reaching does the danger begin. In part, at least, this book is being written for those students. Perhaps it will be up to you, if you are a Christian, to see that they read it. But perhaps, more pertinent than that is your need first to think through the *real potential* of your own life. What is it? Is it clear?

Have you "caught on" that the real initiative is with God? Is the God you know *alert* enough to invade your dilemma, even when you are content to coast along, ignoring Him in the central issues? Is He a God in motion toward you? For that matter, is He a God in motion toward the students who are seeking Him without knowing that it is He they long for? Your *highest potential* is irrevocably tied up with theirs, if you have seen human life through the eyes of the Son of God. How can you, how dare you, dwell only on *your* potential, thanking God that you are not among those who bob along rudderless, and confused? Have you ever thought seriously about God's world-consciousness? If so, why is it that almost anyone who has visited both Christian and secular campuses will tell you that, generally, there is more world-consciousness among the secular students?

Your individual life potential is all-important to God. But so is the life potential of every person in the world. God did what He did in Jesus Christ because, *from the beginning,* He "so loved the *world.*" He did not just begin to love it as Jesus hung on His cross. This was God breaking through into the mainstream of human history, so that we could all see that He has been, from the beginning, *world-conscious.*

If it is true that God created all human hearts alike, then it is equally true that every human search, however misguided it may be, is basically a search for Him. He created us to belong to Him. Your own *real potential* will be achieved with much more facility *if* you have come to an active awareness of your part in the potential of your classmates, your working associates, your friends, the people who make up the "world" in which you live.

I feel I must say here that I do *not* consider you, as young people, to be thoughtless, empty-headed, self-willed, spoiled brats. Some of you are, no doubt. But the majority of today's young people — Christian and non-Christian — are thinking big, sweeping rings around the young people of my generation! We adults have handed you an unbelievably complicated and panic-stricken world in which to spend your future years — in which to discover your *real potential.* We have made a genuine mess of things. We sigh with relief as we manage barely to maintain the precarious *status quo.* "*This week,* anyway," we boast, "man is not going to destroy civilization." And yet, even as I confess our failure to you, I find myself feeling strangely confident because my old age is in *your* hands. As with the three friends to whom I dedicated this book, you have proved to me that you *want* to discover the answers. I don't necessarily think you are better than my generation at your age, but I do believe you are thinking far more seriously.

Take time out in that good thinking now to evaluate your potential; but make this evaluation relate to the potential in the lives of those who make up your "world." We are directly responsible for the climate we create around us. Is it one in which God has access to other people? What about the atmosphere around you? Does it repel? Or does it attract people to truth, as you know it in Christ? I am not speaking now primarily of your *potential* as a "soul-winner." I believe we draw people to Christ by what we *are*, much more effectively than by what we do. If you are realizing your own highest potential, you are doing it because of the presence of Christ in your life. Other people will be won to Him, as a result of His control over you. Winning people to Christ in the daily round is a result of the Christian's progressive reaching toward his own real life potential in Him. We cannot really imitate Him, but we can allow Him to be Himself *in us*. In this we are, as Paul expressed it, "pressing toward the high calling (the real potential) in Christ Jesus."

The young people who seek to find themselves through ways other than the Christian Way (Christ Himself), are bobbing about rudderless, but they are seeking. Too often they do not know what they seek. In their inner beings, they are goal-less. We who follow Him have our goal — Paul's "high calling." The outcome of a life lived toward Christ is mathematical in its certainty. If He is in charge of you, you *will* reach your highest potential. It may not seem high, if you insist upon comparing yourself with someone else. But with Him, for *you*, it will be real.

What do you now think of God, as you read this last chapter? What do you now know yourself to believe about Him? What do you now think of *you*? Have you caught an opening look at the tremendous potential of your life linked with His?

What about His world? The one He created and died to redeem? *Is it your world, too, now?* Have you caught hold of its need for *you*? Has an awareness of the world's need alerted you to interest? Are you ready now to forgive your parents and your friends for their mistakes, and to give them your understanding and your love? Are you interested in taking your place now — as a potential problem-solver, no longer a problem?

Has something new come alive in you, so that you almost hear a shout from the depths of your being: "Come unto Me, I need you?"

Are you ready now to be free? As free as the Son can make you free? Are you eager now to get to work, making creative use of all the energy you've wasted in the past on self-pity and rebellion?

Do you feel a hunger growing in you to find out more and still more about what God is really like? Is there a new objectivity invading your mind? An objectivity which allows you the freedom to see yourself as you *can* be with Jesus Christ at the center of your attention?

Perhaps *you*, who have not yet exchanged lives with this Jesus Christ, have read all the way to the last chapter, and at this moment are aware only of your deep, intensified *longing*. You can know Him, too. Anyone can. That very stirring within you now is His doing. It is His pressure on your heart, and that pressure is your *cue:* Your cue to take the step of faith that will begin a new life for you. An eternal life, in which you can find your highest personal potential, *minus* guilt and confusion. That longing within you is Christ Himself saying to *you:* "Come unto Me . . . I am the Way, the Truth and the Life." I warn you, you will not be able to analyze *how* this first step of faith enables Him to "make all things new" for you. If you could analyze it with your mind, it would not be faith. But once you have begun to respond to His call to you, *you will know.*

If you have never entered into an eternal relationship with the God who created you, you can do it now, right there, as you hold this book. You may say aloud, or even *think:* "Jesus Christ . . . God, here I am. I need You." You will find Him saying in response, "Here I am. I need you too."

This God, this Jesus Christ, has high stakes in all of you who are young. His hopes for you are high, because He knows you as you are. They are high, also, because He knows His intentions toward you.

He alone knows your full potential, with your life linked with His. It is totally His idea that you face yourself as you are, and Him as He is, because with all the energy of His God-heart, He wants you to *find out for yourself.*

CPSIA information can be obtained
at www.ICGtesting.com
Printed in the USA
JSHW021023090321
12388JS00003B/149